TO: Ness

GOD Bless

I wish you all the Best.

Eva miller

The Mysteries of Eva Miller
REVEALED

EVA D. MILLER

iUniverse, Inc.
New York   Bloomington

The Mysteries of Eva Miller Revealed

iUniverse books may be ordered through booksellers or by contacting:

iUniverse
1663 Liberty Drive
Bloomington, IN 47403
www.iuniverse.com
1-800-Authors (1-800-288-4677)

Because of the dynamic nature of the Internet, any Web addresses or
links contained in this book may have changed since publication and
may no longer be valid. The views expressed in this work are solely those
of the author and do not necessarily reflect the views of the publisher,
and the publisher hereby disclaims any responsibility for them.

ISBN: 978-1-4502-3522-8 (sc)
ISBN: 978-1-4502-3523-5 (ebook)

Printed in the United States of America

iUniverse rev. date: 06/10/2010

*This book is dedicated
To my Birthmother Jeannie Hammond
And my daughter Adinah McGhee.*

CONTENTS

INTRODUCTION/PRELUDE

I would be lying to you if I told you that I knew very much about the woman known as Jeannie Hammond. However, one thing I can tell you is that she is my biological mother. Yes, she had me. I was in her womb preparing for a journey one could never have foreseen. A life filled with surprises and shrouded in mysteries that have spanned from one end the country to the other. My name is Eva Danielle Miller and this is the story of my life.

I feel like I need to share my story with the world. Many of you may ask "Why?" or "What makes you so special?" I'm glad you asked. Well, there are others out here that are either dealing with or have dealt with similar scenarios. I really just want them to know from the bottom of my heart that there is indeed hope. I also want them to know that it's ok to question certain things in life in the quest to find out who you really are and where you come from. You may look in the mirror and ask yourself why you are the way you are, and most importantly what your purpose is for being here. I know I have and on my journey I've come to learn that we are all here for a reason. The Most High does not make any mistakes.

I really would like the readers of this book to take away hope and inspiration. It's one of the main reasons I chose to share my story with you all. Never give up on life or your dreams. You can do anything in life if you just put your mind to it. No matter what you've been through in your life or may be experiencing at the moment, always know that all it takes is a spark in the darkness for light to shine through.

They always say that in order for us to be able to know where we are going that we must first have knowledge of where we have been. Many of us have led our lives shrouded in mystery through no fault of our own. That is why this saying is so relevant to many of us out here trying to search for who we really are. We have been searching our entire lives both internally and externally. History always tell the story, this begins the story of my life.

CHAPTER 1
It All Began in California

I barely knew the woman named Jeannie Hammond. To be honest, I didn't even know her for a week. My mother and I were separated after only three days together. You may wonder how this happened. Well, in order to know, we must go back to California in 1980.

Jeannie Hammond lived in an apartment in southern California back then. I believe it was Perris, California to be exact. She was a single black woman who was already mother to a little girl before she became pregnant with me. From what I have gathered, Jeannie tried her best to make ends meet. She was a country girl with her roots in southern Georgia who had moved out west. Sometimes it is an overwhelming adjustment coming from one end of the country to another. The cultures are quite different in various regions of the country. It takes some people years. Others never truly do adjust to a new lifestyle and culture. I believe this was the case with my mother. Everything she was exposed to was different than it was back in Georgia. I assume that she eventually succumbed to hard times and it became more and more difficult for her to sustain herself and her baby girl at the same time. Once she got pregnant again with me, I assume it just became too much for her to shoulder financially.

Now, Jeannie was good friends with the woman who owned the apartments she was living in while she was pregnant with me. I believe this relationship was the catalyst that changed and rearranged lives forever. I was told all my life that there was an arrangement made

e two of them. This woman whom I speak of, my mother's
, her name was Eva. This is who I get my name from. She had
ghter named Danielle and she did not have any children. As I
erstand, Eva and Jeannie had a talk one day. Eva offered to take me
om Jeannie after I was born. She would pay Jeannie for me. She told
Jeannie that her daughter would raise me and give me a better life with
them. Jeannie agreed to this arrangement, to give her unborn daughter
to her landlord Eva's daughter Danielle to raise as her own. The months
passed by and on September 18th, 1980 at 5:53 A.M., Eva Danielle
Miller was born. Jeannie Hammond had given birth to a healthy baby
girl. The last name Miller is where the mystery begins. This last name
would alter my life forever.

Danielle had a boyfriend at that time. His name was Charles
Miller. He was a hulking man. He stood about six foot five and weighed
close to three hundred pounds. His presence was very domineering
as well. This would be a method of control he would use for many
different situations. He is the man who signed my birth certificate. It
was a part of the arrangement that he would do so. My last name was
originally supposed to be Hammond although I assume they wanted
it to be Miller for legal purposes. I spent a total of three days in the
hospital with Jeannie Hammond. Those would be the first and last
three days I would ever spend with her.

When it was time for me to leave the hospital, Danielle and Charles
came to pick me up. Danielle's family was fairly affluent so they bought
a lot of items for their new addition. I was told that I had a good life
with them and that we lived in a nice house, etc. I can only draw from
what I have been told as I was too young to remember the days when
I lived with Danielle and Charles.

Being too young to know what really happened and just being a
baby looking for love, I clung to Danielle as my mother because she
was all I knew. However, there was someone else out there who had a
desire to know who I was, Jeannie Hammond.

It was said that Jeannie had second thoughts about the decision she
made to give me away. From what I understand, I was about two years
old when Jeannie came to talk to Eva and Danielle. She told them that
she really had second thoughts about what she had done and asked if
she could have me back. This obviously did not go over well with Eva
and Danielle and they refused to return me to Jeannie. Danielle told

Jeannie that she would never give me back to her. On the other end, Jeannie told Danielle that she would never give up trying to get me back. Later in my life, Danielle told me that Jeannie never came back after that day to ask about me.

Aside from Danielle dealing with my mother for my custody, her home life wasn't going very well either. Danielle and Charles' relationship had really begun to unravel over the course of time. It was 1983 and I was about three years old when Danielle and Charles ended their relationship. This would signal significant changes in everyone's lives and it was the beginning something that would stretch for years to come.

CHAPTER 2
From One Coast to Another

Danielle and Charles really began to hit a wall. Often times, a new addition can create a strain on relationships but the tension was not because of me. There were a number of issues they had before I even entered into Danielle's life. They argued a lot and Charles would make a lot of threats to Danielle. He would say that when he left, he was going to take me with him. I don't believe she ever took his threats seriously. However, she did make it known that she intended to raise me.

Eva, on the other hand, took what he said very seriously. She told me later on in life that she had never actually liked Charles. She always told me she could see some darkness in his personality. As their relationship got progressively worse, Charles even went as far as telling Danielle to give him some money or else he'd be gone with me. She refused to give him any money. What happened soon after would change everything.

One day Danielle came home to find that Charles' clothes were no longer there. Charles had also packed up all my clothes. She looked for me and discovered that Charles had indeed taken me with him. A small child not even three years old yet had been kidnapped by a man who was just the boyfriend of her adoptive mother. They were not married or even engaged. He wanted to use me at leverage to extort money out of the family. He also knew that with his name on the birth certificate as the father, he would not get into trouble with the law.

Charles was a cunning man. He knew that even if he didn't get any money out Danielle he could get money for just being my guardian. This event was the first turning point in my very young life. Already, my life had been disrupted twice in the course of just a couple years. Only this time, it would take me to the other side of the country. I would not see Danielle again for a very long time. In the meantime, poor Jeannie would not be able to even begin to find me if she ever tried to do so.

Charles ended up transporting me all the way across the country from Los Angeles, California to High Point, North Carolina where his family lived. About two weeks after we made it to North Carolina, Danielle and Charles were in contact. She told him that she was pregnant with his child. I believe at this point she no longer attempted to arrange for my return. I also think she still loved Charles and deep down and she was glad to be carrying his child. The pain she felt from losing me must have subsided because she knew she had a baby on the way therefore she chose to leave me with this man. With Danielle now pregnant, Charles had a link to Danielle and her family's fortune once again. He would have his own child with Danielle.

In the meantime, Charles had already put his strategy of passing me off as his child into action. He told his family that I was his daughter that he had me when he was in California. He also told them that he and Danielle were no longer together. They believed this is was why he moved back. This was one of many lies to come. The man was a really good liar and apparently they believed him. He convinced his mother Patty to look after me for a while until he was able to find a place to stay. Shortly after he had gotten me settled in, he left and told me he would be back soon.

Charles' mother's Patty was a nice, church-going lady. We called her granny. I still have vivid memories of my time living with Patty. The more I lived with her, the less I thought about Danielle. It was not because I didn't miss her. I simply didn't have her presence there. I had been there in High Point for about four months and the memories of that time period were more positive than negative. However, those negative ones really stuck out in my mind.

Patty, Charles' mother treated me well as far as I can remember. I was kept up pretty nicely. I recall seeing pictures of myself in nice dresses and my hair was done. Much of this was done because that family spent so much time in church. In High Point, North Carolina, one big part of the culture there is church. Everyone went. It was my first time ever seeing anything like it. Here I was in what I now know to be the Bible belt of the country attending a southern Baptist church service about two to three times a week. By this time my birthday had passed. I never really understood what was going on because of my age. Nevertheless I really did enjoy being there. It was there that they would tell us about God and how powerful He is; the preacher said that He is always with us and people would nod their heads in agreement and say "Amen". Everyone always seemed happy at church. I loved being in that atmosphere. A big reason was because of the choir. It made me feel good to hear the choir sing. They sounded beautiful to my youthful ears. The music even gave me chills from time to time because it sounded so good to me. Many of the songs made my wonder about Danielle for some reason. A few of the solemn melodies of certain hymns would bring out my young emotions and I would think about her. I had been thinking about her more consistently and I really started to miss her. I didn't have any type of mother figure in High Point. Patty took good care of me but it just wasn't the same.

CHAPTER 3
A Special Encounter

In the meantime, I had decided to make the best of the situation I was in. I had really begun to like going to church and I decided I wanted to join the youth choir. Granny took me to choir practice and I had a chance to be around a lot of different kids. I met a lot of her grandchildren at choir practice because they were all in the choir. They could all sing very well. Charles' mother told them that I was their cousin, Charles' daughter from California. By this time, Charles had gotten his whole family to buy into the lie he had elaborately conjured up. If you ask me, I believe his brothers and sisters all knew what the deal was. Charles had also told me they were my cousins. I was too young to discern things at the time and honestly it felt good just to be a part of something. It really helped to ease the loneliness I felt within.

I embraced them all as my family. After all, Charles was my father and since he was gone I wanted to get to know everyone else. One thing I learned while spending time with them was that they all shared a common bond, music. By going to choir practice with them, I began to become more familiar with music myself. I was fascinated with it. They had a very good choir at the church that was well known. They would often go out of town to different churches, mainly around the South, and the choir would perform for them. I had so much fun traveling, visiting new places, and seeing new venues. We went everywhere from South Carolina to New York. These were happy times with the family. It was not without its gray days either though.

Even with all the fun events that we did and the places we traveled, there was something about life in North Carolina that just didn't sit right with me internally. I was around these people and had what many would consider a family. However, I always felt deep down as if I didn't belong or was not truly a part of it. I was always sad internally and really didn't understand why. They all noticed and would always make comments like "Don't worry. Your daddy will be back soon." or "You miss your daddy don't you?" I know that faint thoughts of Danielle still dwelled in the back of my mind as well, yet it was deeper than that. I felt like I was missing some sort of connection. Through all of my mental contemplation, I tried to keep my focus on church life. It was solace for me in this time of my young life.

Church in North Carolina was different than any place I can recall, especially for a small child growing up. I can recall seeing events that initially seemed exciting to me. However, later on they became more and more peculiar to me. I would watch people who would be sitting calmly until the music grew louder. As the sounds from the drums and organ reached a fever pitch, people would bolt out of their seats. Then they would either start shouting or running all around the church. I always looked on in amazement and wondered to myself "*What is wrong with them*?! " I was told this was a good thing, so for years I just passed it off as such. This was life in High Point.

It had been quite some time and Charles had not returned yet. I always wondered where he was and what he was doing. It was as if I knew I needed a certain presence and had hope that something was over the horizon. After all, at this point I was old enough and conscious enough to know that I didn't have a mother around. This really began to stick with me and even at four years old, I started formulating questions about a lot. I was too young to really project them. Still, they were beginning to form in my mind.

I believe it was during this time period that I went through yet another significant event that would shift my life yet again. The day is bit fuzzy but I can remember enough to know what happened. I was playing at Granny's house with one of her granddaughters. We were both around the same age. We were playing in the living room and we heard a knock at the door. I went to the door and opened it. When I opened the door, a woman stood there and said 'Hi!". She had a very inviting presence. I can recall seeing this woman and it was as if time stood still. We both looked at each other for what seemed like a very long time and then she asked me "Do you want a piece of candy sweetheart?" It was then that Granny came in and told me and her granddaughter to go in the back room while she talked to the woman. After a while, the mysterious woman left the house and shortly afterward, I can recall Granny saying it was time for us to leave her house.

This was an extremely significant moment in my life. I came to find out years later that this mysterious woman who came to visit on that day was none other than Jeannie Hammond. Yes, my birth mother had found me and had come to get me that day. I was told that she knew she had made a mistake when she sold me to Danielle and she was there to take me back home. I was too young to remember her face however I'll always have the memory of being given that piece of candy. I felt a connection with that woman that I cannot explain to you all. It was very strong and to this day I remember it. That strong connection would play back in my mind for years to come.

It was a few days after Jeannie's departure that Charles came back to High Point. He had been gone and working out of state as a truck driver in Ohio for quite some time. His mother had called him and told him that Jeannie had come to her house and attempted to kidnap me. (Now that I'm older I still examine this situation and get upset. To this day, that infuriates me. How can someone kidnap their own child?)

He told me that we would be moving to Ohio. He had met a woman in Ohio while he was working and she agreed to let us move in with her. Having to move just added on to the sadness and distress I was already feeling. I had finally adjusted to life in North Carolina and I would have to adjust to somewhere totally different.

Here I was, on the move. I was on my way to another region of the country. All I can recall about the trip was that it was extremely long. I was drained also emotionally about many situations. I was really struggling with the fact that I had to leave. In my mind, I felt as if I had been taken away from someone I loved yet again. First it was Danielle. Now in my mind I was being taken away from the woman I had come to know was my grandmother. I didn't really know very much about Charles either. It was very awkward because I had been with his family more than him. I really didn't even know this man. We didn't spend much time together. He was gone almost the entire time I was in North Carolina. My young mind was shrouded with so many conceptions and feelings. "*Where am I going now?*" I thought to myself. "*I don't even really know this man. He says he's my daddy so I guess he is. Everyone else has been saying he is.*" Thinking about that, coupled with wondering where in the world I was going to be living next was overwhelming. All I could do was hope for the best as we drove closer and closer to our destination. Charles kept trying to reassure me that everything was going to be fine and that he loved me. "Don't worry about nothing Eva. Your daddy's gonna take good care of you!" He told me that we would be living with a new family in Ohio in a town known as Hamilton.

We'd finally made it to Hamilton, Ohio after what seemed like an eternity. It was 1985 when I arrived there. Already I had lived in three different regions of the country, this time it was the Midwest.

We arrived at an apartment complex, which was a different living situation than I what I was used to at granny's house. I walked in with Charles and he introduced me to a woman named Wanda. He told me that she was my new mother. I looked at her and she was a fairly tall woman. She was a nice-looking, light-complexioned woman and she wore glasses. Her demeanor seemed pleasant. "Hi, how are you doing Eva?!" she said to me. All I could do was look at her. I could not even answer. My mind was in another place. I was very detached at this point. Here I was looking at this woman who Charles just told me was my "new mom". I was young yet I had enough sense to know that this woman wasn't my mother. There were quite a few other people in the apartment also. Wanda had a total of five children. She had four boys and one girl. They were all older children, at least teenage or fully grown except for one of her sons. His name was Eric. He tried to reach out to me though I was not very social at all. He tried to play with me many times although I was not a playful mood. I was trying to mentally adjust to so many changes that all happened so rapidly. It created a lot more complex emotional situations for me. This may sound like a broken record to you all but anyone who has been constantly moved around at a young age can understand and identify with the situation. This change was not an easy transition for me at all. For one thing, I did not know where I was now and even more importantly I really had not had the chance to get to know Charles yet.

Eventually, I started to talk to Eric a little more as days went by. I was glad I did because Eric definitely helped me out a lot with this transition. The only thing that made me feel a little better was having someone around my age to play with. As I got to know him a little more, we found out that we had a lot in common. We were both born in September. Our birthdays were actually only two days apart. We also discovered that we had something a bit deeper in common. Eric's father had passed away before his birth and therefore he didn't have a father in his life. I felt like I could feel where he was coming from because I did not have my mother in mine. It helped create a relaxed vibe between us and helped me continue to open up a little more. We became like brother and sister. I began to contemplate that perhaps life in Hamilton may not be as bad as I first thought. Only time would tell that story.

CHAPTER 4
On the Move Again, the Early Years

In the beginning, life in Hamilton as a child was actually kind of fun in many ways. We had a lot of fun times. Charles would take us all fishing. Everyone would have such a grand time just out there on the water. Charles was still driving trucks and he was gone on the road a lot. He always took us places when he was back in town. However, as time progressed, life at home changed dramatically.

The same good times began to transform into crappy ones. Charles had also begun to exhibit a side of himself that I had never seen. He was no longer the fun, pleasant person who enjoyed taking Eric and I places. He was much more sour and bitter and it showed with everything he did. His entire demeanor gradually became very cold and nasty. He would mix in flashes of his more charming and pleasant side. It was hard for me to figure which side was really him at times. He made us do all kinds of chores at only 4 and 5 years old that we really shouldn't have had to do. The apartment stayed dirty due to so many people constantly coming and going. Everyone from close family to distant friends used to come through that little apartment. We tried to keep it as clean as possible even though that was a hard task with so much traffic. If the place was not clean, we would hear Charles' loud tirades about how we didn't do what he asked us to do. "I thought I told you two to make sure the dishes were done and you didn't do shit while I was gone!" He hadn't even been gone thirty minutes sometimes when he'd tell us to straighten things up. I believe he enjoyed exerting his presence on us and telling us what to do. Because we were young and intimidated, Eric and I gladly did what he asked. After all, this man towered over us. With us only being about five years old, we were terrified of him. He seemed like a giant taskmaster.

The main reason I was so afraid of him was because of the consequences for not cleaning anything the way he preferred. He would take his belt off and beat Eric and me both if everything was not to his liking. We are talking about serious physical contact. This 300 pound man beating a little five year old girl took its toll on me more than just physically. Even at a young age, I felt like it wasn't right. It felt like he would beat us like we were grown sometimes. We used to constantly have whelps from the belts when Charles was done with us. I bare a couple of scars to this day. There were times when my behind literally burned from the beating. This physical abuse was bad enough and it didn't stop there. As I said, things took a turn very rapidly.

Charles would be verbally abusive toward us as well. The phrases I can call to mind the most are being called a "stupid motherfucker" and "a dumb ass". This had a profound affect on my self esteem later on in life. Here I am in a strange place and the only person who is somewhat familiar to me and in saying he's my father, is treating me terribly. This is not what I expected when he told me we were moving here. I was still really getting to know him because he was always on the road in when we were in North Carolina. I was not gathering a good impression of him at all.

As I laid in my bed at night, I would often weep and pray to God to help me and bring me my mother back because I didn't want to get anymore beatings. I started to feel alone again in Hamilton as time passed. I tried to escape what was going on at home through school though I didn't have many friends there. It seemed like girls were jealous of me for some reason. I assume it was because I was the new girl. I really tried to reach out and make friends. I met some over time. Most of the girls still didn't really talk to me. None of this mattered to me though. I liked going to school. It served as a retreat from the crazy life at home. Almost every day after school was like going to a job and Charles was the enforcer.

Even through all of this turmoil, the Most High always provided me with good times as well. I found out Wanda's sister, Hilda, had a daughter a year younger than me and her name was Wynnette.

Sometimes I would go over Hilda's house and spend the night with Wynnette on the weekends. Being over there with Wynnette provided a lot of tranquility for me. It was like I had somewhere to go away from the craziness at home. Hilda lived in a really nice house and I really enjoyed going over and playing with Wynnette. We would always play with Barbie dolls together when I came over. She was an only child so she had a lot of different ones to choose from. She even had the house and all the clothes and accessories. It was a lot of fun playing with her. I enjoyed playing with her also because she had toys to play with that I knew we couldn't afford. Far beyond the toys, I genuinely had a good time every time I came to play with her. It was good for me to have a female friend who was close to me in age that I could talk to. Hilda's house instantly became my favorite place to go. I even got sad every time I had to leave.

As time went on, life at home started to pick up. I had been living there almost two years at this point. Charles seemed to be back to the Charles I remembered when we first moved to Hamilton. He had eased up on a lot of the yelling and though we still had chores, we didn't have to do as much as before. He was taking Eric and me fishing again and we were all having fun again. I loved to go fishing as a child. I was definitely a tomboy. I also loved to catch frogs when we went and even dug worms for bait. I used to do all this every time we went. For the most part everything was going really well for a while. However, it's amazing how things in life can change in an instant.

One day Charles came home and told Wanda that he lost his job as a truck driver. From that point, it seemed like everything went from bad to worse. They did not have enough money to pay the rent. We eventually ended up getting kicked out of the apartment. I came to discover later that the apartment was actually located in the housing projects of Hamilton, Ohio. Once again, I was filled with a lot of sadness and anger. I didn't have a clue what was going on. All I knew was that I was supposed to put my clothes and toys into boxes and that I was not going to see any of my friends that I had just made anymore. Charles said we were moving. I was about to relocate yet again.

I wondered where in the world we were going next. Wanda said that we were moving into her Aunt Mable's house because they did not have enough money for a new place yet. When we got there, I saw that the house was much bigger than the apartment we lived in. It was not long after we got there that I discovered that we would actually have to live in the basement of the house. I was really sad when we moved into that place. The basement was dark, damp, and cold. No matter how bright the light bulbs were in the basement, it had a dark and dim feel to it. Spiders were very present in the basement. You could also feel random cold drafts at night. Charles and Wanda had a talk about the conditions and agreed that it was best to have Eric and myself live upstairs because we all simply could not sleep in that basement. So here I was, in a new place once again and I was about to make another attempt to try to settle and deal with the new conditions I was thrust into.

As with many changes in our lives, moving definitely took some time to get used to. There was a store on the corner of the neighborhood called "Mr. King's" and Eric and I would go there all the time and buy candy with money we got from Wanda. Over time, I began to adapt to where I was. I had started to meet new friends and church was very close. I only had to walk a block to get there. I was starting to become optimistic. That all changed once again on one cold winter night.

I was asleep in the bedroom with Eric. We had both finally adjusted to being at Aunt Mable's house and it was pretty comfortable. All of a sudden, Eric and I were awakened by the sound of two people yelling back and forth with each other. As I sat up, I heard the voices get closer and closer. It was Charles and Wanda. They had come home from a night at a club known as the Legion and they were both pretty drunk. At first we couldn't hear them until they got closer and closer to us. "Shut up bitch!!" I heard Charles yell to Wanda." I won't shut up Charles. You can't tell me what to do!!!" Wanda retaliated. The next thing you know, it seemed as if time stood still for a moment. There was a brief silence after what seemed like a loud pop prior to Wanda telling Charles she wouldn't shut up. Charles had balled up his fist and clocked Wanda squarely in her mouth. She started bleeding immediately. She burst into the room where Eric and I were and yelled "Look Eva!! Look what your daddy did!!! Look!!!" I was bewildered at seeing this grown woman bleeding from her mouth telling me that Charles did this to her. I was absolutely terrified of him at this point. I felt like if he could do that to a grown woman, what could he do to a little seven year old girl like me?

In the midst of this calamity, Charles told me to gather all of my clothes and toys. Wanda was yelling at Charles downstairs and telling him to get out. He told her that we were leaving. Wanda was standing down there with blood on her shirt and mouth as Charles gathered a few belongings. The entire time she yelled at him to leave and called him various profanities. Eric helped me to gather my things as we talked. He was sad too on a lot of levels. He had just witnessed his mother's mouth looking like that. Then on top of that, I was leaving. "I'm gonna miss you Eva." he said. I told him I was going to miss him too. "We'll see each other again." I told him. I gave him a hug and went downstairs.

I was scared and did not want to leave. At this point, I came to expect having to move. All Charles told me was that we would be going back to Granny's house again in North Carolina. I was so tired of being moved and I was hoping it was not going to be as bad this time. At least I was heading back to somewhere I was familiar with.

Charles dropped me off in High Point and he was out on the road again. I really did not adjust nor try to. I was already growing more and more frustrated with each move. I was in North Carolina at granny's house for quite a while. One day Charles showed up at Granny's house and told me that he and Wanda had made up and that they had gotten married. I was not thrilled to be moving yet again. Even at my young age, I knew that all this moving around was not very good. He said he was my daddy and he knew what was best for me. So it was back to Ohio once again. Here we go.

CHAPTER 5
Questions About Myself

I was almost nine years old at this point. As a result of so much moving, I really started to have confusing cognitions about a lot in my life. I thought about a lot on the road when we were driving back to Ohio. I was so confused because I was too young to understand much of what was going on. I always asked a lot of questions. Even at this point, I held on to faint memories of days when I was very young. I even thought about the woman who came and gave me that piece of candy when I was in North Carolina the first time. I really felt connected to her for some reason. On top of this, I had just about formed an opinion about Charles and his character. I was tired of moving. I told him that I was not happy and that I was tired of moving place to place. "When are we going to stop moving around? I don't like having to always go somewhere new." I said. He told me that he had made new arrangements and that I didn't have to worry about anything this time. "I have a new job a lot better than the old one Eva. Everything's alright now." He also said that a lot was going on and going to happen. Time would tell as to whether or not this was true. I had grown skeptical of some of his words.

When we got back to Ohio, Charles had a house for us to move into. I was happy that we didn't have to live with Aunt Mable anymore. Charles told me I had my own room in this new house and that we also had a big back yard to play in. I was very enthusiastic because of the new house. I was hoping we would be there for a long time.

I went inside Aunt Mable's house and Eric was there. I was really happy to see Eric. I gave him a big hug because I had really missed him. He really was like a brother to me and now that Charles had married Wanda, I felt like we truly were brother and sister. I also gave Wanda a big hug when I saw her. I remembered all the kind gestures she did for me when I came to Hamilton. Wanda would always do my hair nicely and lay out my clothes for school. She definitely played a role in helping me adjust to life there and observing Wanda do a lot in her daily routine helped to lay the some of the foundation for the woman I am even to this day. I saw her cook and do all types of other things. She was a clever woman. I would also observe her as she put nice makeup on to step out with Charles. She was very pretty to me and I liked watching her put makeup on and do other feminine things like painting her nails. It was good to see her because it taught me some things about femininity. It was good to see her too.

There were boxes all over the place. I found out that we would actually be moving the next day. I left all of my belongings packed that I brought from North Carolina. I was pretty tired from the ride and I went to sleep to get ready for moving day. As I laid there in the bed, I thought about the move as I drifted to sleep.

I woke up the next morning ready for the day. Charles had rented the moving truck and everything was packed. We left Aunt Mable's and drove toward the new house. Eric and I were very anxious to see what it looked like. It was over on the eastside of town. The address was 510 East Avenue. We pulled up to it and I liked what I saw. The house was big, yellow two story structure. It had a nice porch also where you could sit. I went inside and immediately ran upstairs to see my room. I was so happy to have my own space to play in. Eric's room was right next door to mine. We moved everything in and got settled into life at the new house.

It was 1990 at this point. I have to admit, my early memories of life in this house were very nice. Charles was even being kind toward everyone and he wasn't yelling at Eric and I like he was at the old house. We had to go to a new elementary school called Jefferson Elementary. I was in the fifth grade now. I liked our new school and I met a lot of friends at this one. I was actually in a good place mentally and just happy to have a new start. I just wanted to be happy.

I thought with us moving into this new place that home life would finally become more stable and we would not have to move anymore. During this time, I became more involved with school activities. I felt that maybe I had finally reached a point where I didn't have to move around so I got involved in band at school because I loved music. I wanted to play the trumpet and I even told Charles. He was very happy for me because he was a musician. Honestly, he wasn't a bad one either. He could play several different instruments. He had been involved in various bands since early in high school so he was able to help me learn how to play. When I was in band class, I always went into a blissful state that I couldn't really explain. The music took me to a different place.

When we first moved into the new house, everything was very good. Most of all, it was peaceful. Before too long, it started to go downhill in a lot of different aspects. For one thing, Charles was not very good when it came to finances. He wouldn't pay the water bill on time and the water would be cut off at home. He would come in from the casino a lot and I'm sure that had a lot to do with why the bills were not getting paid on time. Even when he did pay one bill, another was neglected so we remained in the same predicament with a different utility. We saw many days with no lights. Winters in Hamilton, Ohio could be very cold and a lot of snow was common. One can imagine the brutal temperatures once the wind was factored in. It was very difficult to get through those days without heat.

Over time, I began to observe that Wanda and Charles continuously did a lot of drinking. They still constantly had company coming in and out of the house. They would always be partying and there would be a lot of drinking going on. I could not stand having a house full of people all the time. All of these factors began to wear on me as I was getting older. Charles continued to raise hell at Eric and me because the house was not clean, yet it was him that seemed to do all the entertaining.

Charles' inability to handle money had a big affect on me in the process. There were times when he couldn't afford to buy me any clothes. I was growing into a young lady and there were items I needed. I was thankful that through it all, the Most High always put certain people in my life to help me out. There is one person in particular that forever sticks out in my mind. Her name was Eleanor Bailey. Wanda's brother had a girlfriend named Toni and Eleanor was her sister. I was introduced to Eleanor and I immediately liked her. We instantly had a bond. She was aware of a lot of events going on and she and Toni used to take me shopping and do things for me to help me out. Eleanor also did hair and she would do mine sometimes. She truly was an amazing woman. I had tremendous respect for her. She had been through a lot of adversity in her life and had persevered. Eleanor was diagnosed with cystic fibrosis at nine months of age. They told her she wouldn't live a normal life however she was able to do everything everyone else did. She was an inspiration. I enjoyed my time out with her and Toni. The clothes they bought for me made me feel a little better about going to school because I knew I looked nice. I was really quite shy at this point in my life. Internally, I always wanted to be social. I believe I always felt as if I truly never fit in. That was a factor in why I felt so alone at times. Eleanor, who I would come to affectionately call Aunt Deenie, would also let me come over and clean her house for her. She would pay me and I enjoyed spending time with her and making a little money on the side. I could buy myself a nice dress or something with the money I earned and I liked being able to do something for myself. I was learning vital skills that I would need to carry for years to come.

After I came home from school or a friend's house, I would always find myself cleaning up the aftermath of the company Charles and Wanda had the night before. It was nothing new. I hated when they got drunk because that's when they would argue all the time. At times I felt like he would then take his anger out on Eric and me. I can still recall many nights in which we were awakened around three in the morning to his drunken voice. He would wake us with his usual drill. We would march into the kitchen and Sergeant Charles would point out whatever it was we didn't do. We remained "stupid motherfuckers who couldn't get anything right." Then he would take off his belt and ask us which one of us wanted to go first. Eric would always go before me because he knew I was scared. I always had love for him for that. He knew that by the time Charles was done with him, he'd be tired when it was my turn. These situations made Eric and I even closer because we were both going through the same thing and understood where each other was coming from. I got really tired of being around negative people and situations. On top of feeling alone, my self esteem was suffering. After constantly being called dumb, sometimes it can really affect your outlook.

As much as I loved Eric and respected Wanda, I began to formulate in the back of my mind "*If this was my real family, I would not feel this way."* I knew they were not my real family and that always stayed with me in the back of my mind. They had a connection that I just did not have with them. I was in a phase in my life where I had started thinking about my family and its history. I didn't know anything. My origin was transforming into a mystery before my very eyes. I was starting to have more questions than answers. I would ask Charles questions about myself. "Who is my mother? Why haven't I seen her?" "Where was my mother's side of the family and why did I never see them?" I asked. "You want me to tell you? Ok I will." he replied. "I'm gonna tell you about your mama." He started telling me the story. "I met your mama back in California. She lived in some apartments I used to hang around." "She was down pretty bad and I could tell she needed a little help." He went on to explain how he got to know her. He said he learned that she was on drugs and he felt sorry for her. "Over time, I really started to care about your mama. One night I went to see her and one thing led to another." "About two months later, she told me that she was pregnant and I immediately knew the baby was mine." He also said that he got with Danielle while she was pregnant with me. "We knew we could give you a better life so I told your mother I wanted to have custody of you." "After you were born, Danielle and I took you home with us." He went on to tell me that eventually he and Danielle started having problems. "Yeah, things started turning cold between me and Danielle. Her mother really didn't care for me either and I never did anything to her." I decided to leave the situation and start me a new life. Since she was not your real mother, I decided to take my baby with me and that's how you ended up in North Carolina." I was listening closely to everything he said. It made sense to my young mind. He told me that the woman I remember as Danielle was actually my adoptive mother. "Your mama's name is Jeannie. Jeannie Hammond." I couldn't believe what he told me. He said he didn't know where she was and that's why he didn't really talk about her. Hearing this information was a lot for me to handle. I also asked him if he had any baby pictures of me because I always wondered why I never saw any pictures of myself as a baby. I always wanted to see them and he didn't have any at all. Charles said the ones he had burned in a fire while I was in North Carolina with his mother. All I could do was take what he said for what it was.

This information changed everything for me. Hearing these revelations opened my mind to entirely new thoughts and scenarios.

At night I would pray and ask God to help me find my mother. I wanted to meet her so much and thought of her often. Many questions about her began to form in my mind. *"What did she look like? Was what daddy said about her true?"* I didn't care if it was. I really wanted to put the face with the name. I wanted to find her.

I was very unhappy during this time, dealing with all of this internal and external conflict. Not knowing who I really was began to have effect on me subconsciously. The only time I had fun was at school. As usual, I found an escape within the school walls everyday. I was there with my friends and didn't have to deal with anything at home. However, my grades suffered greatly. It was hard for me to focus on my homework many nights because of either arguments or company. Either way, there was always noise and distraction. I did just well enough to get me by each of my classes. When the report cards came in the mail, Charles would just yell at me and call me dumb. It would make me so sad and I would wonder *"Why does he talk to me this way?"* When he was really upset, the belt usually wasn't far behind. After being punished, I would go to my room and cry. I grew ever so tired of the issues going on in my life. Thank goodness I had my friends at school. They seemed to be my only bright spot and many of them lived in the same neighborhood.

Of all the friends I had at the school, two people stood out the most and I became really good friends with them. There names were Shonika and Shani. We hung out at school all the time and did a lot together after school. You could always find us spending time together. Everyone at the school knew we were best friends. They called us the "pretty girls". One day at school we were sitting at the lunch table eating our lunch and I saw a group of boys sitting on the stage they were six graders. I saw a boy name Damekeonnus. He stood out to me. He was so cute to me. I couldn't stop looking at him. I noticed he was looking at me too. So later that day we saw each other in the hall way and we started talking to each other. I noticed that he dressed very nice and he was short like me. We both liked each other so we became boyfriend and girlfriend. I was so happy that I had a cute boy friend that was my first boy friend and my first love. When I would see him he would always have on new shoes and clothes. (I believe his mom spoiled him.) I couldn't wait to get to school everyday so I could see him.

The summer was almost here and we were getting out of school.

My friends and I were so happy. One day Shonika and I were walking to the store and we saw Damekeonnus. He was with his friends, and he told me that he was moving to the other side of town. I was sad because I wouldn't see him anymore. He told me that eventually one day we will run into each other again. That was the end of my first little crush.

It was summertime in Hamilton and sixth grade was fast approaching. I was happy to stay up late and be able to sleep in. It was fun playing with my friends all the time. Wynette would also come over from time to time. The nightly chores at home continued but it was nice to not have to at least go to school. Charles would be Charles. I can recall a time over that summer when Wynette and I saw Eric eating some candy. "Where did you get that candy from Eric?" I asked. "It was in the freezer so I just picked it up." he said. Little did he know that the candy actually belonged to Charles. He had a petrified look on his face as I told him who owned it. A little later that night, Charles went to the kitchen. He looked in the freezer and yelled "What the hell happened to my got damn candy?!!!" He was drunk so we knew it was going to end bad for Eric. He confessed to Charles that he ate it. Eric was called the usual "dumb motherfucker" and was met with the fury of Charles' belt for eating it. It's crazy that these are the type of memories I can recount with ease.

Summer came and went as did the school year. It was more of the same constantly going on. Graduation from elementary school came fast I was happy to graduate. I felt good because I made it through regardless of the many issues I had to deal with. Aunt Deenie came by and took me shopping to get a beautiful dress for the occasion. I can recall that dress vividly. It was a nice pink dress with a sequence flower on the side of it. She also did my hair and together with the dress, I definitely looked and felt a bit older. I was so blessed to have her around. In my mind, this graduation was just a stepping stone. I was preparing for a totally new moment in my life, junior high school and another new beginning.

This was a summer of immense anticipation. I was turning into a young lady and teenage years were right around the corner. All my friends and I were charged about junior high school. Shonika and I couldn't wait. I spent a lot of time with her and Shani. We'd go over Shonika's house a lot and hang out. Shonika also had a brother who was really cool to me. His name was Tone and he was friends with

Eric. I would actually hang out with Tone myself sometimes. We all could not wait to be around older kids. I was beginning to go through puberty and I had begun to like the boys. The night before the first day, I could barely even sleep. So many scenarios were going through my mind about the new school. I wanted to be liked and to fit in. I didn't know what to expect. I woke that next day, got dressed, and did my hair. I was ready for my first day at Garfield Junior High School. More importantly, I was ready to enter a new step in my life.

CHAPTER 6
A New House, a New Start

I met up with my friends Shonika and Shani and we walked to school. The school district did not give us a bus route because the school was in walking distance of our neighborhood. We made it to the building and I could tell school life would be different. It was a much bigger building than Jefferson Elementary. Once we got inside, we had to find our homeroom classes. The school was so big to me and I loved it. It was a totally different vibe and I was ready to meet new people and have fun. Lunch time was different at the new school. I saw my friends and I was able to sit with them and talk about all of our new classes and teachers. Of course we also talked about all the cute boys we saw. That first day was excellent. I really enjoyed it and junior high school started off really well for me.

Being the music lover that I am, I got involved in band again. I had enjoyed it in elementary school so I had a feeling I could in junior high also. I met a lot of friends in band. A lot of people in the band class were fun to me. They accepted me as a fellow band member and that was a good feeling. The class was enormous compared to the size I was used to. It was ok though because I liked new scenery and was able to embrace it rather than look at it as a negative. I gave it my best no matter whom else was around. Our band teacher was very nice and down to earth. His name was Mr. Airnoff. His wife also worked with him. Together, that duo made band class some of the greatest times any of his students could remember. A lot of people at school had the perception that people in the band were all geeks. I honestly didn't care what anybody thought because I loved music. Being in the band introduced me to different genres of music I wasn't used to listening to. Some of my band mates would have music ranging from metal to classical and I would listen to all of it. I would apply it and play it myself sometimes. My passion for the music grew a lot during this time in my life because of the exposure to so many different sounds.

I also wanted to be involved in anything else I could that interested me. I tried out for the drill team and made it. I was so thrilled. I was having a superb seventh grade year in junior high school. I was meeting a lot of people and was pretty popular. Boys started to notice me and I was really growing into myself and happy for a change. After school activities were also a big part of school life. Home life was always the one thing that brought me back to reality.

The school year came and went rather quickly. It was summertime again in Hamilton. I had finished up my first year of junior high and had done very well. It was more of the same at home. Bills were not getting paid and different utilities would have service disconnected. Aunt Deenie still came around to help me out every now and then. She was always a breath of fresh air. As always, Wanda did everything she could. I appreciated everything she tried to do and respect for her remained. She always found a way to make something happen and I liked that about Wanda. Summertime ended just as rapidly as the school year did and before I knew it, it was time to go back.

It was 1995 and I was going into eighth grade that year. Over time, Shonika's brother Tone and I started hanging together a lot more. He became like family to me, like a cousin of sorts. I still had a lot of love for Shonika. It simply seemed as we got older that we just began to go our separate ways. We began to explore life on different paths.

Tone and I would go to church every Sunday together and we also sang in the choir together. Church continued to be a big part of my life as it always had been. God has always been the most important thing in my life. Tone eventually grew to become my best friend and we were always together somewhere. I don't believe I had ever truly had a best friend until Tone came along. He was someone I actually deemed trustworthy and vice versa. He was very compassionate about my plight and I could tell he really cared.

It wasn't long before tensions at home went from a simmer to a boil.

It was like some sort of sick pattern that had developed. Charles came in and announced that we would have to move out of the house. I was livid. We'd have to pack up everything again. "Where are we going this time?" I asked him. He said he had another house for us across the railroad tracks for us to move into. When he said that, I already knew what area he was referring to. The different sections of the city were all pretty much divided up by railroads tracks. Everyone in Hamilton knew that "across the tracks" meant into the most disenfranchised areas of Hamilton.

Hearing this news left me feeling gloomy again. This had been the most stable environment I had been in up to this point. Every time I made new friends and got used to being where I was, we always had to relocate. I hated this "pick up and go aspect" that had come to plague my life for years. I really started to dislike my dad even more for this. I discerned in my mind that he was the main reason my life was like this. If he would have just paid the bills, then we would not have had to always move somewhere else. In my mind, I began to question his fatherhood abilities. *"What kind of father would put their child through something like this all the time?"* I would often ask myself. I rarely had peace of mind outside of school and deep down I still felt displaced, as if I didn't really even truly belong in Hamilton, Ohio period.

We moved to the new place on the other side of the tracks into a house on Chestnut Street. It was not nearly as nice as the last house. I had no choice but to make do. I continued to attend Garfield Junior High however that was short-lived. They found out that we were living in the new location, outside of Garfield's district. Therefore I had to transfer to Wilson Junior High. I didn't like it at all. As I stated earlier, the area we moved to was not known as a good one and I did not really want to make any new friends again. I was just getting burnt out with it at that point. The landscape was different than where we previously lived. Right down the street from the house was a spot known as the Square. That was where a lot of people would go to buy and sell drugs. There was also a store called "Mr. Singletary's" right by the square on the corner so there would always be traffic coming and going on that tiny strip. This was my first time being exposed to this type of environment and I stayed to myself for a while when we moved to this neighborhood. I missed my friends from the old neighborhood a lot, especially Tone.

All of this made me consider a lot about my real family believe it or not. Bad situations made me think about my mother. I would think about a lot of different things. *"If I was with my mom, I wouldn't be going through this right now."* I would say. I'd also wonder *"Did Jeannie have any other kids besides me? Did I have any aunts or uncles?"* Many internal questions began to manifest within me as I became more and more introverted. This time period gave me a chance to really get back into myself. I was formerly involved in a lot of activities in school so this was a good time for me to analyze aspects of my life I had not addressed in a while. I wasn't as social so I was able to become a lot more contemplative. I prayed that Jeannie was out there looking for me and that she would find me one day to take me away from all this chaos. I was feeling a lot of pain inside that a lot of people could not see. I was fourteen now and honestly did not know who I was. During this time, I continued to withdraw and become more introspective.

Life at Wilson Junior High was not fun at all. On top of missing my old friends, I was not really meeting many new ones. I met a few here and there although not nearly the volume of those at Garfield. A good friend to me at Wilson was a girl by the name of Cassie. She was a cheerleader. She was very friendly and she made life a bit easier for me at Wilson. Eventually I decided to pursue some type of activity after school. After all, the new neighborhood we lived in was nothing like the last and I really did not want to spend much time there. I decided to join the basketball team. It was about the only thing that I really wanted to do and I figured it could help me fit in a little more. I was right. Being on the team was actually a pleasant experience. I met a lot of people playing basketball. It was fun going to other schools and seeing how they looked and play games in different gyms. I had to practice a lot and I was fine with it. Practice kept me away from home. I remember coming home from one practice in particular to some news that would change the course of my life for years to come.

I had come home from a hard practice and Charles called me into the living room. "I just got off the phone with your granny and she said she talked to Danielle." Danielle had found her. Honestly, at this point I really didn't remember who she was. It had been a very long time since I had seen this woman. Once Charles told me about my biological mother, my only thoughts were of Jeannie. I knew she had me and that was who I wanted to see. I asked him to remind me who Danielle was because he had passed her off to me as just an ex girlfriend. He said she was the woman who he was dating when Jeannie gave me away to him. He went on to say that we lived with her in California before we moved to North Carolina. He said that in a sense, she was my mother because she was there for me when I was a baby and took care of me. Charles also told me something else. "You also have a brother Eva!" He told me that he had a twelve year old son with Danielle who was my brother. He asked me if I wanted to meet Danielle and their son whose name was Wade. My intrigue would not let me say no, even though it was a lot to soak in. Perhaps this woman could give me some more insight into what was really going on and answer so many questions that had materialized over the years. *"Maybe she knows where my mom is."* I told myself. Only time would tell. It was arranged that we would meet in North Carolina in a couple of months at Granny's house. I was actually very enthusiastic about meeting them. I was going to meet my "adoptive" mother and my brother I never knew I had for the first time.

CHAPTER 7
A Life-Changing Experience

I was fifteen years old at this time and was really coming into myself more and more. I was at that point in life that all teenagers go through, trying to figure out who I really was. I would often look in the mirror and examine myself and think *"I don't look like Charles at all."* As a child, he would always go to lengths to convince me that we looked alike. Every time I told him how I felt about it, he'd always try to point out that we had similar noses and eyes, etc. He was delusional to me at times. Either way, all I could focus on was meeting Danielle. I was very hopeful that she could give me some insight into my past. Maybe she had some answers for me about Jeannie too. Charles really didn't seem very enthusiastic about the meeting. I thought that was weird for someone who'd never seen his son before. Deep down, I had begun to have bad qualms about the story Charles was telling me about my life and began to ask myself *"Does he not want to go because of what I could potentially find out about myself?"*

In the upcoming time before meeting Danielle and Wade, I just went to school. I tried to make some new friends in this new neighborhood eventually. It turned out to be a repeat of my experiences from the last neighborhood. The girls around there didn't really like me very much either. I began to fight a lot with them. I knew they only tried to fight me because of jealousy. I was the new girl and it was all about them trying to establish themselves and intimidate me. Little did they know I was not the type to back down from a fight. Because of these events, I didn't associate with them. Living conditions in that neighborhood deteriorated pretty quickly and I was glad I was leaving for a while. I just didn't want to be in Hamilton, Ohio anymore. There was nothing in Hamilton for me. Opportunities were scarce and people had always told me that one often had to leave that place to have a better life. I suppose it's all about perception. I knew had bigger dreams that reached far beyond Hamilton's city limits and I planned to reach them no matter what. I was ready to head back to North Carolina.

We rode the Greyhound bus to get there. It was Charles, Eric, and I. I was glad that Eric went along for the trip. The bus stop was in Cincinnati and the ride to North Carolina was long. I had a funny feeling inside I couldn't explain. I was very eager though. I felt like this encounter could change my life. The only thing on my mind was meeting my adoptive mother and my brother. "*I don't really remember her but I am looking forward to meeting her.*" I thought to myself. I also thought about Wade as well. "*I can't believe I have a brother. I hope we can be cool and have a good relationship.*" The ride to North Carolina was long and quiet. After many hours we had finally made it. We got our bags and waited for Granny to pick us up from the bus station.

It didn't take long for Granny to get to the station. She arrived and Danielle was with her. I walked over to the car and saw Danielle for the first time since I was a toddler. She was a tall, light-complexioned woman with long hair. She wore glasses also. She gave me a hug and immediately started shedding tears. "What's wrong?" I asked. She replied "I've missed you for a long time and I'm just glad to see you again." I really didn't remember her because I was too young to materialize any of my days with her. Nevertheless I was glad that someone out there cared about me. Seeing her show so much emotion made me really want to get to know her again. Her vibe came off really warm to me. Charles got to meet Wade for the first time also. As I looked at them together, I could definitely tell that Wade was Charles' son. They had similar features and mannerisms. He was just a lighter version of Charles and just a little slimmer. As I talked to him, he seemed like a nice young man. He was smart and I could tell he had been raised well.

We stayed a few days in North Carolina and I had a decent time. It was good to have a weekend away from Hamilton and the constant bickering between Charles and Wanda. I wanted to talk to Danielle about a variety of things. I never got the chance though because so much was going on. I did let her know that I wanted to see her again. She told me that if I ever wanted to come and live with her, her home was always open to me. I was glad she said that because I would definitely take her up on her offer sooner than later. *"I'm going home with her tomorrow."* I had concluded. I told Charles that very same day that I was going home with Danielle. She told me that she lived in Florida and I felt like a nice change of scenery was exactly what I needed. Charles and Danielle talked about it and he said that I could go. I was thrilled. I couldn't believe that this would have happened on this trip. I was ready for a change. Goodbye projects, hello palm trees.

I went down to Florida with Danielle with only the items I brought along for the trip. The scenery was way different than anywhere I had been to before. She lived in a small country town in Florida known as Blountstown. It was about 40 miles outside of Tallahassee. I was there for the second half of the school year. She treated me very well. It was a major contrast from what I was used to living with Charles. There was always food and nothing ever got cut off. She was very responsible and I really looked up to her because she always handled her business. The only people that lived in the house were her, Wade, and me. Her mother Eva also lived in Blountstown not too far from us. I had gotten pretty comfortable and didn't really even get around to addressing the dilemma with my past and Charles. I was just glad to finally be somewhere in which I could have some peace of mind. I was thankful for the chance to go somewhere else and collect my thoughts. It was short lived though as I had to move back to Hamilton only six months later. It was agreed that I could always come back. I thanked Danielle for allowing me into her home and treating me well. I had never received anything like that before from a guardian. Also, I got really close with her mother Eva before I left. I was going to miss her a lot.

CHAPTER 8
Projects and Front Street

When I got back to Hamilton, it was as if I had never left. Everything was the same if not worse. A year had passed and Charles still wasn't paying the bills. He would often borrow money from friends. The problem was that he would not pay them back so he burned multiple bridges. No one would give him a single penny. This all eventually led to us getting evicted yet again. At this point in my life, I had simply had enough. I was sick of this and had grown even angrier at these circumstances. We had nowhere to go and no money. I felt like a nomad constantly drifting to the next destination. This time was worse than prior moves though. Wanda's daughter Billy had a place in the projects. She told Charles we could stay there until he found a place. We had lived in a house right outside of the projects. Now we'd be moving right in the heart of them. I'd have to put up with these crazy females even more so. Not to mention the environment around me. I didn't have anywhere to escape to.

The apartment was very small and it was only a two bedroom place. Those conditions became very crammed with six people living there. I hated it. I had to share a room with both Wanda and her granddaughter. I slept on a mattress on the floor next to a bed. All of my clothes were in garbage bags. Everything else I had was put in storage. It was hard getting used to the way of life here in the projects. I wasn't used to it and it was hard to adjust to. At least when we lived on Chestnut and

I would hang out down in them, I could leave and go home. Now, we were right in the middle of them twenty four hours a day.

As time passed, I became more social with people in the neighborhood. My theory is that over time they began to feel like I was no different than they were. It was hard for all of us living in an environment were poverty was noticeable at every turn. School continued to alleviate my stress, as it had always done. I was so glad to be back in school. I was in the ninth grade now and I would be going to high school soon. I was still social at school, befriending everyone from band members to cheerleaders. I just had one of those personalities that was able to socialize with people from different walks of life. I was starting to rebel against Charles' authority also. I felt like he couldn't really run a household when he didn't even have his own place. I started to care less about what was going on and more about hanging out with my home girls. I was a teenager trying to find herself and that journey would take me down a lot of different paths.

That year I graduated from Junior High School and was headed to high school next. I was still hanging out with my home girls, trying to escape from my sad life. One night we were all standing outside and we all decided to smoke weed. Everyone else around us was doing it at the time and we were curious. We would get together and smoke at night. Smoking weed didn't come naturally to me. I had to learn how to inhale and once I did, the entire feeling changed. I liked the mellow, hazy feeling that came to shroud my mind. I liked smoking it because it took focus off many of the problems going on in my life. Honestly, I had begun to become a product of my environment at this point. Living in that area started to influence my behavior after a while. The hood had started to tap me on the shoulder and I was answering. Deep down, I understood it wasn't right yet I did it anyway. It wasn't long before I started drinking. Smoking and drinking together made that summer go by really fast. At the end of that summer, Charles told Eric and me that he had some good news. He'd finally found us an apartment. We were so thrilled because we would finally be leaving the projects and we'd finally have our own rooms again. At least I could go into high school with a room of my own. It was not a good feeling sleeping on a mattress in a roach infested apartment. We packed up what we had over Billy's house and grabbed everything out of storage and moved into the new place. This was a move I had no problem making.

The new place was actually right across the street from the projects in a newer development known as the "new homes". The living arrangements were a little better than those at Billy's house. We had a three bedroom and having more space was definitely easier on everyone. However, Charles and Wanda's house continued to be party central and someone was always spending the night. They played their instruments like they were performing in some club. Charles and some of his friends had a band known as "Dice" and they'd constantly practice. It was as if everything had picked up right where they had left off in the old place before we had to move in with Billy.

I was almost sixteen at this point and I was not nearly as accepting of the conditions as I had been as a little girl. I was a very tidy and clean person living in an environment that was constantly dirty. Wynette would come over and see me sometimes. One day she told me that she had gotten a job at the McDonalds uptown and that she was making her own money. She told me they were hiring and I walked uptown to put in an application the very next day. It all went well when I got there. I actually got an interview from the manager that same day and was hired. I was ecstatic. It was my first job. I went home and told everyone that I had a job. Charles acted as if he was ecstatic for me. Shortly after telling him, he told me that I would have to give him some of my check every time I got paid. Hearing this really put a damper on my mood about the job. I was finally going to be earning my own income, only to give this man an undeserved portion of my hard earned dollars. I was going to high school in a month and I needed to make as much as I could. Overall, I was happy that I would be making my own money though. In my eyes, it was a step toward independence. I was glad to be able to buy myself some clothes for school. As the summer came to a close, I enjoyed going in to work and having fun when I was off. The summer had finally come to a close and high school was only days away.

CHAPTER 9
School Days, and Band Life

The first day of high school was a totally different experience from junior high. Hamilton High School was immense in comparison to the junior high school I just had come from. There were so many people there. From my first impression, I liked the school and I felt like I would fit in there. Working at McDonalds, I was able to do a lot more for myself. My entire style and wardrobe changed, and I was able to keep my hair done all the time. Guys started to take notice of me and honestly, I liked the attention. I was really starting to come out of my shell. My confidence level was at an all time high.

Band remained a big part of my school life and I joined the marching band at Hamilton High School and started playing the baritone horn. I loved every minute of it. Many of my band mates from junior high had also joined. It was fun being with them along with the new students. Our time to shine was Friday night at the football games. Whenever Friday rolled around, everyone in Hamilton knows that is football night. When we put on those blue and white uniforms it was show-time. We played at every home and away game. The entire vibe of Friday night for a high school football game was unlike any experience I had prior. There was not much to do in the town so everyone showed up to them. The games were very big in the community and the community was very involved. Everyone went out after the games. On our side of town, there were a few small clubs in the hood that we would all go to. One of them was the American Legion and another was Mahogany's.

Mahogany's was more catered to the younger crowd and that's where we often went. I would often stay out until two and three in the morning after a game on Friday nights.

At this point in my life, I had pretty much begun to do whatever it was I wanted. I was sixteen now. I really wasn't listening to much of what Charles had to say. Gone was the timid and shy little girl that I once was for the most part. I had become a lot more confident in myself and had gotten past a lot of the verbal abuse that I had endured as a little girl. Home life was not really much more than me coming home to get sleep, preparing myself for work and school, and being in my room for homework, etc. Even with all the turmoil I had going at home, I made sure I made it to school on time. I didn't want to miss any days because I didn't want to miss band. I loved it. I especially loved away games because it was a chance to travel and see other cities and towns. More importantly, it was a chance for me to get out of Hamilton. On the outside, it seemed like I was having a lot of fun, though internally I was yearning for much more. My life's vision was so far beyond the city limits. I had a family out there. Part of my dream consisted of finding them and I realized I would have to leave Hamilton one day to do so.

I had come to a place in my life in which I was becoming increasingly conscious of the world around me. As I looked around Hamilton, the vibe of the city grew more desolate by the day. I had come to learn that Hamilton was a town that housed many secrets within its limits, secrets that one could probably deem indescribable. Many people in Hamilton, Ohio I was associated with had not ever even been outside the state of Ohio. Most had lived there for their entire life and didn't have any plans on leaving. There were not many opportunities in that town and I was determined not to become stuck there. I comprehended deep down that I would never find out the truth about myself and my family if I stayed hidden away in this small city outside of Cincinnati that few knew about. Hamilton itself wasn't a bad place to settle and raise a family if things were steady. It just didn't fit with the course I wanted to take my life in. The theme of leaving played in my mind over and over again. I had come to the conclusion that I would have to leave Hamilton to achieve those dreams. I just had to figure out how.

In the meantime, I continued my routine of going to school. I met a good friend in school that I clicked with and befriended quickly. Her name was Amy Harbrecht. We actually met randomly in the hallway on the way to class one day. Our lockers were near each other but we had never spoken before. She came up to my locker and said "Hi my name is Amy. We have had lockers near each other for all this time and I don't even know your name." 'My name's Eva." I replied. She didn't look like she was from Hamilton. She looked like a California girl like me. She was about 5'8 with blond hair and blue eyes and she had a nice tan. "You're pretty." She said. "Thanks, so are you. You look like a Cali girl." I told her and we started laughing. That day was the beginning of a wonderful friendship. Amy and I had our own style. Wherever we went we turned heads. Yep, we we're a dynamic duo. She was one of the most down to earth people I had ever met and she had a lovely family. I appreciated her friendship and we are still friends to this very day.

Meanwhile, I continued the same routine I had been doing. Working and going to school were the main aspects of my life at the time. After a while, it became very mundane to me. Something deep inside me was not at peace. Internally, I was seeking much more. I had begun to feel as if I was slipping into the drab abysmal routine that had sucked so many in and made them complacent. Some of my friends from childhood were now mothers. I didn't want that for myself. I had to get out of this place.

Conditions in Hamilton had transformed a lot since I had first arrived many years ago. There was a lot of violence and some people I went to school with were now in the ground. We were all only seventeen years old and some of our lives had already been cut short before they started. I didn't want to go down this path. I had to formulate something. I concluded that I needed a change of scenery. *"I can't stay here and be a part of this. I have to find a way to leave."* I told myself. That's when I remembered my conversation with Danielle. She told me that I could always come back anytime if I wanted to. I decided that I would come back to Florida and the only difference was that this time it would be permanently. It was time I gave Danielle a call.

CHAPTER 10
New Life in a Small Town Called Blountstown

It was spring time and I felt it was the perfect time for me to leave. We did not have a phone at the time so I used a payphone across the street to call Danielle. There was no answer when I called. I waited until the next day and called again. I got no answer. It did not matter to me because I had made up my mind that I was leaving. I would just surprise Danielle instead. *"I'm gonna say I talked to her anyway."* I told myself. I informed Charles that she said I could come and he bought it. Over the course of the next couple of weeks, I had saved up enough money to get a bus ticket on the Greyhound to Florida. I anticipated starting a new life with a new family. At the same time, I was very afraid and anxious about it. I did not know how she would react to me showing up unannounced. All I could do was pray about it and that's exactly what I did. I felt better after that and I knew that I would be doing the right thing. The path my life was on was not a good one and I needed to remove myself from this atmosphere. My time in Hamilton, Ohio was done. I was leaving it behind along with many memories that rest inside me, both pleasant and unpleasant. I would only come back here to visit. I was headed to another small town. It was back to Blountstown, Florida.

The bus ride was extremely strenuous. With the multiple stops, it took about twenty two grueling hours to get to Blountstown. I slept most of the time, trying to pass as much of it as I could by sleeping. I had finally made it to my destination. I gave Danielle a call and no one answered again. I was starting to wonder if this was the right number. I began to think *"Had she changed her number? Was she still in Blountstown?"* I called the number once more and she finally answered. I told her that I was at the bus station in Florida and she came to pick me up. She was taken back to see me and asked me how I got down to Florida. I told her everything on the ride home, from how my life was going in Hamilton to how it was just time for me to get a new start. "I need to be around more constructive people and surroundings." I said to her. When we got home, I was able to lay it all out on the table and tell her what really happened during my time in Ohio. Her mother Eva was also sitting with us, listening in on the conversation. I really liked Eva. We all talked for a long time and I disclosed to them all of the memories of situations I had gone through there. I filled them in on Charles' alcoholism and how he drank often. They learned of how poor we were and how we had to live in substandard conditions because of Charles being irresponsible with finances. I let them know that he was both verbally and physically abusive when he drank. I held nothing back and it felt good to finally let someone know what I had been dealing with. They both looked disturbed as if they could not believe many of the stories I had told them. They were both furious. Danielle told me that I never had to go back to that lifestyle. She looked me in my eyes and told me that I could move in with her. She said "Eva, as long as I have a place, you do too." Hearing her say that gave me a good feeling. I was also relieved. I prayed about it and God had made a way.

Danielle's mother Eva was thrilled that I was living with Danielle. I could tell that she missed me and she told me so all the time. One thing she always said to me was that she always believed I would come back. I didn't really understand what that meant at the time. I was starting to become more and more curious about that. After all, many aspects of my life remained shrouded to me and the only information I had was what Charles gave me. I knew my mother's name was Jeannie Hammond and that she'd given me to him to raise with Danielle. He had told me that since he was my dad, it was ok and for the best because at least I would have one of my parents. I had made up my mind one day to ask Eva why she said that to me.

Living with Danielle and Wade was much better for me. I had my own room again, only this time I actually had my own bathroom also. That was something new to me and I enjoyed that. The house was a nice three bedroom and very spacious. Danielle had a pretty nice career with the State Department of Revenue and honestly, she had a lot of nice things I simply was not used to. The only drawback of living with them was Danielle's husband Verne. She had gotten married since the last time I had seen her and he was a bad choice in my opinion. I didn't trust him and I could tell he didn't like me very much either. In spite of him, I really settled in and I was enjoying the changes in my life.

I grew very close to Eva shortly after moving to Florida. She had expressed to me several times that she couldn't stand Charles and that she has been very angry with him for years. I just assumed he had stolen some money from them or something. Charles was a money hungry person after all. However, I never asked why she was.

I liked Eva's personality because she was no nonsense and straightforward. She just told it like it was. Danielle would sometimes sugar-coat what she said; Eva on the other hand other hand, would give it to you raw. I had a feeling deep down inside about her. Something inside of me felt like this woman may hold the key to a lot about my past. We shared the same name and her daughter's first name was my middle name so that immediately made me think about things. "*I know this isn't purely coincidental.*" I thought. I genuinely grew to love her too. She was older and lived alone so I would always call her and check on her. I just wanted to do my part to look out for my grandma.

Living back in Florida was getting better and better by the day. I got along very well for the most part with my brother Wade. I was used to having a brother because I lived with Eric in Ohio. We had a lot of good times together. He played high school football and Danielle and I would go to his games on the weekends. I felt like we were really coming together as a family.

Meanwhile, life in Hamilton seemed to continue to try to exert itself no matter where I was. I gave Charles a call one day to check up on everyone there. He told me that they were going through some really rough times. He said that they got evicted from the apartment they were living in after I left. I felt really bad for Wanda and the rest of the family. Charles always seemed to end up putting everyone in some sort of predicament.

I was very glad I had left and felt tremendously blessed to be out of those conditions. That was a repetitive cycle I was finally out of. I felt like the Most High took me out of those situations just in time. I could have easily been out on the street with them. The new life I was beginning to develop in Florida was a far contrast from the life I lived in Hamilton for so many years. I was living with someone who was financially responsible, in a house that was constantly clean, and there were not nearly as many people coming and going as when I was living with Charles. She also had a car and was always able to go where she needed to at anytime. I'm sure these things may seem small or insignificant to some people. When you are used to much less though, it makes you more appreciative. Having a female figure in my life that was accomplishing a lot really empowered me. I learned a lot in Hamilton except this was on a different level. I saw someone who had made strides that I hadn't seen from women I had been around and seeing Danielle do her thing served as an example for me. She was a computer programmer who worked for the State of Florida who had built a nice steady career for herself over the years. As time went on, I felt like I could make strides also.

I started to get really serious about getting myself together and started to formulate a plan. I was going to make sure I made the most of the opportunity that the Most High had given me. I found out later that I would have to go to an adult school just to be able to graduate on time. From skipping school and just going to work some days, I had fallen really behind back in Hamilton. It was the only way because I was a total year behind. I would have to do a year's worth of work over the course of only 6 months. In Hamilton, I would have probably given up but it was different in Florida. No one would tell me that I was stupid and it felt good to be confident in myself without being torn down. I'd get this work done and graduate on time.

Over the course of the next few months I really dug in deep with the school work. It paid off. I completed it and graduated on time with the class of 1999. Finally I had finished high school and I was thrilled. In my mind, I felt like I had finally accomplished something major. Getting my high school diploma did so much for my overall morale. I was ready to take on life as a young adult, liberated from the bonds of high school. Like most people fresh out of high school, I had been thinking a lot about what I wanted to do next in my life. I recognized that I had some talents. I just didn't know what path to go down. This was my first major decision I had to make for myself.

One day I was talking to Danielle and she asked me what I wanted to do. I told her that I wanted to go to cosmetology school. I had done hair for so many girls in Blountstown. I figured that would be a choice path for me to go down and take my skills to the next level. Danielle told me that she would pay for me to go to school. I couldn't believe that someone was going to help me out in such a big way. I was very thankful for her help. I was delighted because Danielle and Grandma Eva were proud of me. It felt wonderful to say I was going to cosmetology school. I was glad to be doing something and most importantly, I'd found a path I wanted to explore.

CHAPTER 11
Do You Wanna Know the Truth?

Life in Blountstown, Florida had gone into full swing for me. Everything was sound for me at this time. Sometimes, I couldn't help but feel like it was too good to be true, like something was lurking in the shadows. It seemed to be this way for me for so long. As I reflected on my journey up to this point, it was evident that a new environment was all needed. I was flourishing and doing very well in school. I went through the courses and I finished them all with high grades. Danielle and Grandma Eva were very pleased. It felt excellent accomplishing another goal. I was shedding all former doubts of myself I had from the past. I even missed Charles sometimes because I knew the state he was in. After all, he was still my dad. At the same time, memories of the past continued to haunt me from time to time but over time those feelings dissolved.

After I finished cosmetology school, I was able to land a job at a salon in Tallahassee. I lived at home with Danielle and since she worked in Tallahassee, I would just commute with her on days I had to work. I didn't have a car and it was an opportune time for us to talk when no one else was around. I finally felt like we were getting closer. Eventually, my feelings for Danielle grew and I found myself calling her mom more than Danielle to the point that eventually that was all I said. I felt she had earned the title.

Over the course of my time in school, Grandma Eva's health began to fail. She was beginning to get sicker and sicker over time. I had always had a connection with her. Danielle and I had one too. The difference between hers and the one I shared with Eva was that it there from the very beginning when I got to Blountstown. We just seemed to instantly click even though I didn't know her. When I used to go check on her, we'd talk for a long time and I found out a lot of interesting history about their family. They were originally from upstate New York. Eva had married a prominent dentist by the name of Carey Wade. He was Danielle's father. They moved out west to California and he had accumulated a decent amount of wealth over time. He passed away years before they had moved to Florida. I grew to love Eva. She was very real and down to earth. That made her very easy to talk to. We had one talk in particular that would change the course of my life forever.

I had gone over there to check on her as usual and we began to talk. I was experiencing one of my days of inner turmoil because I didn't really know much about my past and I wondered a lot about information I did know. So, I asked her if she knew anything about my birth mother and where she could be. She replied to me that last she heard, my mother was in California. My heart raced faster than ever before. Here was someone who actually had contact with my mother and could really tell me something about her. I cannot fully describe how I felt even knowing such a thing. I'll never forget how Eva looked me in my eye and asked in a loud, serious tone "Do you want to know the truth?!" I was hesitant yet I was not afraid. I told her "Yes, I do want to know. I've been waiting my whole life to know the truth!" The information she revealed to me next would change my outlook on so many parts of my life. "The first thing you need to know is that Charles really isn't your father!" I was stunned and shocked at the same time. She told me that he had actually gotten into an argument with Danielle and kidnapped me from them when I was about three years old. Eva told me "You still have family in California Eva! Here let me give you something." She went to a box and opened it. Inside where old pictures that looked like they were taken in the early 80s. "You see this little girl right here? This is your older sister. Her name is Iesha and she is a year older than you." I was absolutely thrown back. To know that I had a sister out there was a joy that I couldn't explain to anyone. I had been around unfamiliar people my entire life and to finally have a link to my real family did wonders for me. "I always wanted you to know about your real side of the family. Charles took you from me so

I never got a chance to share these things with you." She said. To find out that Charles was not my real father was devastating. This man had lied to me for all these years. I cannot even begin to describe the sense of betrayal I felt. I was very angry and this revelation made me recollect about so many different scenarios. After hearing this she told me "You were mine first Eva. Jeannie had made arrangements with me. This is why your name is Eva. I gave you to Danielle because she didn't have any children." It made a lot of sense to me and everything began to come together. I was going through a lot in my mind with all this new information. I had always felt deep down inside that I never truly belonged around him or his family. They had only been accepting to a certain degree and in later years had changed totally. This went a long way toward explaining why. I was enraged as I thought about all the negative experiences in Hamilton because of a man who wasn't even my biological father. He had taken me away from a family only to have me living in substandard conditions, deal with abuse from his alcoholism, and be manipulated by him for years. "I have something else to show you!" she said. She showed me a copy of my birth certificate. I had never even seen one up to this point. It had Charles' name. I saw my mother's signature. It just fueled me to want to find her even more. We sat there together that afternoon and she told me a lot of things about my past. This is why I am able to share the earlier events with you all. I thanked Grandma Eva for telling me this information and I gave her a big hug. I perceived that there was something special about this woman and that she could tell me something about my life. That feeling was correct. It was time to take this new found information and figure out a lot about my life. First, I had some business to take care of. My next step would be to give Charles Miller a call.

Danielle with her mom and dad

Danielle back in the day

Eva and Aseelah in High Point

Eva and cousins in High Point

Charles and Wanda

Eva and Eric in the 80s

Eva singing in church in Hamilton

Eva at church again

On my way to the club

At home in Blountstown, 2001

Eva and Malinda at club V-12

Wade and his family at the graduation

Club Pin Ups Decatur Georgia

Eva and Tone in the ATL!

Eva at the beach

At SirTavion's Graduation, 2006

Eva visiting mom in Blountstown

Eva and Wynette in Tallahassee

My Aunt, Uncle, other Aunt, and Birth Mother (order is exact)

The day of mom's funeral

Eva and Ocie Davis

Season 7 American Idol

Having Fun

CHAPTER 12
Life in a Different Light

I was absolutely furious about these revelations. I went home and called Charles immediately. He answered and before I knew it I was saying everything that came to mind. "Grandma just told me that you are not my real father!" I blasted over the phone. There was a long pause before he answered. "It's true." he said. Hearing this news just broke my heart into pieces. My first question upon hearing this was "So where is my real father then Charles?!" He told me "Your father died before you were born Eva." I didn't even know whether to believe him or not but I had so many other questions for him at that time. I went on to ask "Why did you kidnap me from them?! What was your purpose for doing that?!" I asked him. He just replied with a bunch of excuses. "The reason I took you was because I loved you. Danielle wasn't paying you attention like you think." I was not hearing any of it. I felt at this point like if he lied to me my whole life, one more lie wouldn't make a difference. Upon processing all this news, tears streamed down my face as I just broke down inside. *"How much more deceit would I have to be around? Why was my own origin so shrouded?"* It opened up even more questions for me about my life. The entire time, this man concealed the fact that he was not my father and went to great lengths to brainwash me into believing he was. Again, I began to ponder on the many nights I was exposed to harsh environments and abuse. I got off the phone with Charles and I believe after that conversation he knew that the relationship between us would never be the same. I'd always respected Charles and had truly believed over time that he was my father. I had grown to love this man in spite of the bad stuff that went on during childhood. I even thought his mother was my grandmother. It changed my perception of her, as well as many other family members upon hearing this news.

I was very thankful for Eva. I cannot say that enough. After that day, the level of love and respect for her increased so much. She had given me something in my life that no one had before, truth about my past. We became closer than we ever were. Danielle and Wade took notice of it. I think Danielle was actually upset with her mother about her telling me the truth about my paternity. I could tell their relationship was not the same after she told me. Even though their relationship became a bit tense, Eva and I were both glad that the truth was out in the open. I know I was. It would alter my thought process for the rest of my life because I had more clarity now. I was aware that it would take me a while to sort this all out. At least I had Eva to help me out along the way as I began to unravel the mysteries I had about my past.

It was summertime of 2001 at this point and grandma was not really getting any better. Although she was a strong woman, her health continued to decline a bit. She stayed active even though her health was declining. Danielle always planned a family trip in the summer and one day we all had a meeting about the destination of the trip for that year. Danielle suggested that we go to California to her goddaughter Natalie's high school graduation. She told me it could also be an opportunity to find some information about my real family. Initially, I told her that I did not want to go because I didn't know any of the people they were going to visit. One night she called me into her room with her and her husband to talk about why I did not want to go. They asked me "Don't you want to find your family Eva? California's your birth state after all. If you go to California, we can make arrangements and get some information." I reluctantly agreed. It felt like an excuse they used to get me to come along. "What about Grandma?" I asked. Danielle said that she did not want to go and she would be ok at home and the caretaker was going to watch her over the weekend. I had not been to California since Charles took me, so deep down I was a little excited about going. "Yeah, I'll go." I told them. After all these years, I would be headed back out west.

We drove to Tallahassee to catch our flight to California. The flight was actually relaxing. I had million things on my mind as we flew across the Sierra Mountains. I had so many thoughts surrounding Jeannie and still had some about Charles as well. Mom wasn't off the hook. I had questions for her too. *"Did she know the whole time that I was with Charles? Why did she let him take me? They had to have talked. They have a child together."* My mind raced over and over. Danielle would look at me sometimes and ask me if everything was alright. I knew this was not the time or place for those questions so I just focused on finding out some information about my family.

We landed in Cali, got the rental car, and checked into the hotel. We were all jetlagged from the cross country flight and went to sleep. The next day was very pleasant. We all had an enjoyable time shopping, dining out, and taking in the scenery. California was a lot different than anything I had seen, yet I felt right at home. I took in the warm summer air that day. We had a ball. The next day we went to visit some of mom's friends that she knew from years ago when they lived in the area. Everything was going fine until on fateful phone call.

We were all in the living room when mom asked Wade to call home and check on grandma. He asked to speak to her and he paused for a second. He gave mom the phone. The caretaker told Danielle that Eva had passed away. She told Wade and he came over near where I was and sat down with a blank look in his eye. "What's wrong?" I asked. "Grandma died." was all he said. I couldn't believe she was gone. I was crushed. My heart plummeted to the floor. All I could do was cry. Eva and I had just begun to get so close. She meant a lot to me and it was a heartbreaking loss for me on so many levels. I was thinking *"This can't be happening right now. I know this can't be true."* Mom walked over to me and just said "It's better this way." There was very little emotion or comfort in what she said. From my eyes, as I looked around no one else seemed very sad. I was the only one who cried upon hearing the news. I did not really know how to react to seeing how emotionless they all seemed. I understand that everyone deals with death in different ways. Still, there was something that just didn't feel right to me.

We went back to the hotel and the trip was cut short a few days. Back at the hotel, I was really down. I took this death really hard at the time. Mom came into me and Wade's room and said she wanted to talk to us about it. I thought she was going to talk about how Grandma passed. She actually told us some different news. Mom told us that

Eva had a trust fund for both of us. Honestly, I had no idea what a trust fund was or how they worked. I asked her to explain it to me and she summed it up by saying that Eva had left us some money. I was absolutely floored. Here it was not even twenty four hours after her passing, and here we are already talking about money. At this point, I was just ready to get back to Blountstown so that I could mourn for Eva the way I wanted to.

CHAPTER 13
Dark Times Ahead

The next day I found out that we were actually staying a few days longer in California. This was very weird to me and I absolutely couldn't understand why we weren't rushing back to Blountstown to handle these affairs with grandma. We ended up going to her goddaughter Natalie's graduation as if everything was normal. After the graduation, Danielle said that Natalie would be coming home to live with us and attend college. I was actually glad because there would be another girl in the house. I liked her when I met her so I hoped that we could be friends.

After three days, the trip out west was finally over. We all went back to Florida and Natalie came with us. When we got back, Danielle began to make all the funeral arrangements for Grandma Eva. This was not a funeral I was looking forward to attending at all. Her death was very hard for me to deal with and it would take me a long time to heal from it. It was one of the most surreal

experiences I'd ever had. It seemed at times at if I was mourning more than others who had been around Eva their entire lives. Again, I understand that death is handled differently by everyone. It was just that when I looked at Wade and Danielle, they just did not seem as if her passing fazed them very much. I don't believe I remember seeing my mom shed a single tear at all up to this point. It made it hard to reach out to them about how I felt about it because their vibes weren't very consoling to me. I tried to deal with it as best I could on my own. After about a week, it was time to lay grandma to rest.

We buried Eva in Blountstown. As we stood at the grave site, I saw them lower her into the ground. Along with her went so much history I had left to learn from her. She had shed light on my dark past and now she was gone. I was thankful for her presence though. She told me enough to change my outlook on life for years to come. After the funeral, I was feeling pretty low and decided to venture out. I went to a place down the road called "the cut" where people would gather to drink, smoke, gamble, etc. It was nothing more than a dirt road surrounded by trees with a small hole in the wall club nestled in the back where they would play pool. There wasn't much to do in Blountstown, so I decided I'd drink my problems away and smoke a little weed to ease my mind. This turned into a more consistent thing as time went on. Months had passed after Eva's death and I was smoking on a regular basis, most of the time down in the cut. It was actually one of few places for me to hang out. All the popular guys hung out down there and I knew everyone in Blountstown by this time. I did not really associate with too many females in Blountstown other than doing their hair for some money on the side. I did not want a repeat of my experiences in Hamilton. I got the sense that some of them had some petty jealousy issues as well, so I chose to just stay away completely. I wish it wouldn't have been that way because I was very social and didn't mind making new friends.

I started coming in really late at night. Sometimes Natalie would stay out late with me. Danielle started to take notice of the change in me and noticed the type of company I started to be around. I had also begun to be exposed to powder cocaine down in the cut and I became curious about it. One day my curiosity got the best of me, one of my homeboys asked me if I wanted to try it. "You wanna hit the sack? He asked me. I looked at it really closely and I told him that I would try it. He took out a straw and handed it to me. The first time I tried it, I felt really hyper. My heart was racing and it was as if I was more alert than I'd ever been. It tasted disgusting although I honestly liked the feeling associated with it. It took my mind completely off Eva's death. At the time, I felt like I didn't know what I wanted to do next with my life and cocaine started to become an escape from my problems. I was headed down a dark road and didn't have my headlights on. I had no idea what type of consequences it would have. Eventually it went from trying it every now and then to a growing addiction. What was I doing? Why did I make the dumb decision to even try it? I should have never tried it in the first place. Many days, I would come in from down at the cut and go into my room so that Danielle didn't see me. Natalie never tried it. She would hang out with me a lot. I was glad to have her around during this time in my life. She had similar views of the household that I did. Wade was always gone as usual with his friends and Danielle was always working. One day Danielle came home in a very joyful mood and announced that she had found a new house for us to move into and we all went to go take a look at it.

It was on a different side of Blountstown, in the small affluent section of the town. As we pulled up to it, I was amazed. It towered in comparison to the house we lived in. The lot was very large so there was a good amount of land. The house also had a nice sized pool in the backyard. It even had a slide and diving board. As I looked around, I could tell that it was pretty expensive. It had to be worth more than a half million dollars. "How many bedrooms are in this house mama?" I asked Danielle. "It has five bedrooms and four bathrooms Eva." She replied excitingly. "I figured that we needed a bigger place now that Natalie is with us." I knew then that mom had received her inheritance from Eva's passing. With her being an only child, she received everything, the entire family fortune. We were all shocked when she told us she had already purchased it. It all happened so rapidly. Moving into that new house was going to change everything. The entire lifestyle we were living was about to soon change, and some people along with it.

When we moved into that bigger house, Danielle did not take any of the furniture from the old house with her. Everything she bought was entirely new. I had never seen such spending before in my life and honestly at my age I felt like it was fun to be a part of. She bought everything from nice glass tables to large flat screen televisions. Eva had told me that they had built a small fortune but she was being modest. That "small" fortune was actually much bigger than Eva portrayed to me. At the rate Danielle was spending so freely, there had to be a decent amount. She continued to be financially responsible except the rate of spending was much higher and more elaborate than before. I always had to assume based on what I either heard her say or what she did. I never asked mom how much her mother left her. I felt that would be disrespectful to my grandma.

Therefore, I just sat back and watched. Wade also benefited a lot from the new lifestyle. He was only a junior in high school and Danielle had bought him a brand new Chevy Avalanche, completely paid off. She gave him money for rims and a new sound system and even had TV screens in the headrest. Wade began to change as he was bestowed with so many new items. Danielle did buy me a car too, a used Hyundai Sonata. I was just delighted to have a car even though. I didn't care that it was not the same caliber as Wade's. There were times however when I did feel as if she showed Wade favoritism though. I was not really the type to measure love based on what you buy someone. I was the type that measured it based on actions. Natalie said she noticed since her arrival how Danielle would treat me differently than Wade. She felt as if Danielle showed Wade a lot of favoritism also. It wasn't about the material things but rather everything from the enforcement of rules to simply showing affection. I tried not to mull about it too much. After all, Danielle was my mom and she had opened her house up to me and had given me a chance to get out of Hamilton. Deep down though, I always held in the back of my mind that blood was thicker than water. I started to feel more left out as time passed. It was a golden age for Danielle, Wade, and Verne. Natalie had met a guy in town named Ervin and had begun dating him. For me, I was dealing with a period of turmoil. What direction was my life headed in? I felt like I had everything I wanted as far as material items but as we all know, that alone can't make you happy and content. I didn't want to go down a road of no return. Even though I was doing things I probably shouldn't have been, I wanted to make a beneficial change and do something progressive with my life. I hadn't come to Florida for nothing. It was time for me to figure out a lot about my life and what I was doing. I had a secret I was hiding from everyone and before it got out of hand, I had to get a grip on it. I needed to clear my head and I left the cocaine alone so I could think clearly. I was glad I did. In the midst of everything I had been dealing with and all the changes taking place, I had applied to Florida A&M University. One day I got a letter in the mail from the school and I opened it. I was accepted. I was tense as I read the letter and ecstatic after I did. I was going to college. I wanted Danielle to be proud of me. More importantly, I needed to be proud of myself. I was ready for the journey. I felt my life had finally found direction again and I was ready to travel down that new road.

CHAPTER 14
Collage Plans, and the Best Band in the Land

Life in Florida really started taking off for me at this time. Danielle couldn't have been any more proud of me to hear that was going to college. My experience at Florida A&M started on a fantastic note. I was enjoying every minute of it. Since mom worked in Tallahassee and I went to school there, we'd still often ride together in the mornings. It was valuable time for me because it was always a time of bonding for us. The rides were always peaceful. Eventually, the commute started to wear on us both and Danielle came to me with an idea one day. She said that she would withdraw a portion of the money grandma left me in a trust fund and buy Natalie and I a townhouse in Tallahassee. I could not have been more ecstatic. Not only was I in school, I would have my own place. I was going to be an owner of property at the age of 21. Natalie and I would be roommates and I was fine with that. She was going to be at Tallahassee Community College. I felt blessed like never before, not for the material aspect of it. It just served as an example of how far I had really come in comparison to where I had been. This was going to be a new experience for me and I was ready for it.

Natalie, in the meantime, had started feeling sick more and more over time. She never wanted to go anywhere or do anything. I didn't have a clue what was wrong with her. I told mom about it and all she said was "I'm making a doctor's appointment!" After she said that, I had a feeling what was going on. She took Natalie to the doctor the very next day and they found out that Natalie was pregnant with Ervin's child. Danielle was livid upon hearing the news. Her demeanor toward Natalie transformed from something warm and inviting to one that was cold and distant. "I didn't bring you down here for this. You need to have an abortion Natalie!" she told her. It got pretty heated at this point. Natalie was not receptive to this at all and told Danielle that she was keeping her child. It was then that Danielle told Natalie that she was sending her back out west to California. It was very sad for me because I had a lot of love for Natalie. It was good to have another cool female around, especially around my age. I understood why she had to leave though. It simply would have been too tense for her in Florida. Danielle followed through with what she said and Natalie went back to California. I moved to Tallahassee by myself. I really wanted a roommate. It dampened the move a bit yet I was still delighted about having my own place and I was going to make the best of it.

After I moved to Tallahassee, one of the first priorities I set for myself was to make sure that I stayed focused on school. I was really enjoying FAMU. The entire college experience as a whole was a lifestyle change for me. Many times, I didn't feel like I fit in there only because I was coming from a region in the country that had maybe seven black people in a class of thirty. I suppose life in Ohio was embedded in the back of my mind. I had never been to a predominantly black school at any time in my life. There was so much culture and so much to learn. I imagine I adjusted well because I absorbed a lot of things I carry with me to this day.

Overall, college life was very good. I went to a lot of functions and soaked up all that college life had to offer. However, it wasn't all fun and games. In the midst of making progress, I had also regressed in other ways. Partying was part of my routine and I enjoyed being out and going to clubs. I can recall one party in particular where I met this girl named Malinda. She went to Florida State. She had a great personality and we started hanging out. A lot guys liked Malinda. She was curvaceous with a caramel complexion and she got a lot of attention. She'd often come by the townhouse and smoke weed with me and talk about life. We had a lot in common and had a similar outlook on life. We'd also go out and have a good time. Malinda had one of those personalities that made her easy to talk to and open up to.

I eventually told her about my past and how I had ended up in Florida. She was very sympathetic and told me she couldn't imagine not having her mother in her life. To this day, I know that is one reason why we grew closer as time went on. She understood where I was coming from. I was new to Tallahassee and needed a friend. She became the best one I ever had there. We're still friends to this very day.

Life in Florida was pretty good for me at this point. School was my primary focus. All I wanted to do was focus on school and what direction I wanted it to take me in. Things became pretty mundane over time though. I went to class and came home to my chocolate toy poodle named Napoleon, who I nicknamed Nippy. One thing that both fired up and amazed me during this time was attending Florida A&M's football games. I absolutely loved it. I can vividly remember my first time. Coming from Ohio, I did not know anything about their band. Once I heard them perform at the halftime show, I was completely blown away. It was absolutely spectacular. As they majestically took the field in a sea of green and orange, I stood in amazement at the shear size of the band. I mean this band actually covered the entire football field. They consisted of more than four hundred members. I had never seen a band that size before in my life. Once they began to play, I never heard instruments produce sounds on that level. They also danced as they played their music. This was phenomenal to me. Being formerly in a band myself, it just made me appreciate their sound even more. I missed being a part of it. I really did. The crowd seemed to feed off the energy of the band. They cheered for the band just as loudly as they would for the football team, if not more. I came to find out that the band had a very strong tradition and legacy. They had been around for over one hundred years. The first band formed back in 1892. To start out originally with just sixteen instruments and evolve into the incomparable band that they are today is amazing to me.

Being that I lived in Tallahassee, it was easy for me to go see Danielle for lunch. I enjoyed having lunch with my mom. It was a good substitute for the car rides that we no longer enjoyed together. Everyone at her job knew me and I really liked coming to see her. It was close to campus so I could have lunch with her and make it to class on time. Summertime of 2002 rolled around and I was about to end my sophomore year at FAMU. It was also around time for Wade to graduate from high school. I was proud of him for finishing. Danielle and I sat at lunch one day and discussed it. Usually the lunches were pleasant yet this one had a vibe that I was going to hear something I did not really want to hear. She told me that she had called everyone in North Carolina and told them about Wade graduating. They said that they would drive down to attend. It would be Granny, Charles' sister Janet and her husband, and none other than Charles' himself. I expressed immediately to her that I did not like the idea of him coming. She said that he was Wade's father and she thought it would be nice if he attended. Though I remained angry about his deception, I reluctantly conceded. I was not ready to see this man face to face for the first time since learning that he wasn't really my father. I housed a lot of anger and resentment toward him and seeing him was not going to do anything healthy for it.

CHAPTER 15
Graduation and Contemplation

After hearing this news, my emotions were all over the place. I asked Danielle "So, where is he supposed to be staying?" She replied that she told him that he could stay with me. She knew I did not want him to stay with me. Nevertheless, she knew I would do it because of the way my heart was. I did it for Wade. I just wanted to get through it as quickly and peacefully as possible. She also mentioned that one of her friends we visited in California was moving to Blountstown. Her name was Tina. I wondered why she would want to leave California to come to a place like that. She was mom's friend and I presumed that was a reason.

They arrived for the graduation and everyone came by my townhouse. I couldn't believe that mom actually came by to my place. She worked right in Tallahassee and I had been living there a year without a visit from her. I was infuriated. I felt like she only came over because Charles was there. This was the beginning of a whirlwind weekend.

I remembered the other family members that had come down. The funny thing was that I had met them long before Wade. I really didn't like Charles' sister Janet very much. I can recall her playing on the telephone portraying her self to be my mother when I was a young girl back in North Carolina. How could someone do such a thing? Most of the entire family presented a façade. Granny was still decent to me in my eyes. I continued to give her respect. No matter what she was an elder. I also thought about everything she had done for me as a child. She treated me well enough and I always thought she was my grandmother until I learned the truth. Even when I did, I still loved her. Even with her presence there, I did not feel as if I fit in. Looking at Wade with his family gave me an elated feeling for him yet an empty one for myself.

I never experienced what it was like to be around one's real family members. I began to really long for that. Here I was looking in the mirror, no longer knowing who I was. I did not know who I came from. *"Who did I truly get my features from? Why did I do certain things?"* These questions just added even more mystery to my life's story. It was like the more I discovered, the more I had yet to discover.

The graduation was very nice and I very proud of Wade for making it through high school. It was a very weird feeling for me, being around Charles. I was glad that we hadn't been alone yet. I was not prepared to talk to him even at this point. At one point in time, it didn't seem like Wade was either. I could tell when they embraced that Wade had an air of resentment for Charles not being in his life. I understood how he felt. A young man definitely needs his father. I just thought to myself though *"Wade, if you knew what your father was really about, you might not feel so bad."* Overall, we had a good time that weekend. Even though I felt out of place at times, I enjoyed myself as best I could. Seeing Wade with his family only fueled me to know my own and perhaps even find them. I had avoided talking to Charles all weekend and I was glad that it was coming to an end. I was dealing with so much that my mind was in a flux. I was not focused at all.

Months passed by after Wade graduated. Events were not going very well in my life. Dealing with so many internal issues had an adverse affect on everything I was doing. I thought about my real family more than I had previously and doing so ate at me internally in ways it never had before. School was no longer a top priority for me and my grades began to slip. It got to the point where I was contemplating dropping out completely. I knew this wouldn't please mom, on the other hand that's how I felt. I honestly did not know what I wanted to do with my life anymore. I didn't want t go to school. I wanted to learn more about myself and I really wasn't feeling school at this point. I felt like I was searching for myself and it was time to find her, the real Eva. For so many years, I had been lied to about who I really was that I had come to a point that I really did not know. It hurt so much on the inside to have to bare this. My entire demeanor became less joyous over time as I sunk back into a place mentally that I had not been to since my days in Hamilton. Only this time it was worse because I had so much more insight. I did not really know how to deal with what I had going on so I began to withdraw from everyone and everything. I began to even neglect my responsibilities. For the first time in my life, I really did not care. Little did I know that this attitude would come back to bite me.

One day I came home from school to find a letter about property taxes. I was very nonchalant about it and honestly did not look at it as a big deal. I was a new homeowner and did not understand the significance of the taxes. I discarded it and forgot about it. Just months later I was served with papers stating that I owed back taxes. Since Danielle was the co-owner of the townhouse, she also received the tax documents. She was furious with me for not paying them. She told me that because of this she wanted full control over the house at this point if she paid the taxes. I was unemployed at the time and I really had no choice except to let mom pay it. As a full time student, I didn't work. She paid most of my bills for me. I was going through a lot and not having a job was even more depressing. My life in Tallahassee that had started off so well was now taking a terrible turn. On top of these events, my car began to mess up as well. I did not know what I was going to do. I was growing more and more desperate. I had to formulate something.

One day I thought to myself that I it was time to make some bold moves in my life. I had been so passive that it was time for me do something different. I was tired of being treated as a black sheep. No matter what, I kept remembering that blood would always be thicker than water. I hated to start any trouble or disharmony yet I had to do something. I called my mom and told her that I would agree to her taking full control of the townhouse only if I would receive half of what the property was worth. I felt like that was reasonable because she would be able to sell it easily and I needed to have something to start over with. I was about set to leave Tallahassee. I didn't know my destination quite yet. I simply felt like my time in Tallahassee was growing shorter and shorter. She replied that she would only give me ten thousand or just a tenth of what the townhouse's value was. I did not accept this and I requested fifty thousand dollars. This was a turning point in our relationship. I started to look at her differently and vice versa. I felt like she was not really trying to help me. It really hurt my feelings because I knew that the townhouse was purchased with my grandmother's money in the first place, money that she'd left me. It just made me recall Grandma Eva and how thankful I was that she gave me something even more valuable than any house or money. She had told me the truth, something no one else in my life had done. She gave me a sense of who I was and it was time for me to find out more about that. Ultimately, I knew that I was going to lose the house and so I would have no choice. I had to accept Danielle's offer. A letter came in the mail that made it official and that she was assuming full control of the townhouse. She told me that I had to leave once it became effective. I couldn't believe she was actually evicting me. She felt that the money was enough for me to just pick up and leave. One of the terms of the agreement was that I had to leave everything in the townhouse including furniture. I would be left with only the few thousand dollars that I would receive from the townhouse and I kept contemplating about where to go.

My car was not running very well. It wouldn't make it long distances. I could not possibly move back home with Danielle. The tension was extremely high between us at this point. I had to come up with a plan. One day I was watching TV and saw an advertisement for an audition to be on *America's Next Top Model*. The auditions were going to be in Atlanta. I thought to myself *"I'm going to go try out. I think I have what it takes to be a model."* I had made up my mind. I was headed to "A-town". Aside from wanting to chase my new found dream to model, I also knew that my mom Jeannie was originally from Georgia. I figured this would be my ultimate goal of moving to Georgia and Atlanta would be a good place to start my search.

I met with Danielle and the lawyers and signed all the paperwork. I was issued the check and went back to the townhouse for the last time. I sat and thought about a lot. Only I knew I was leaving and I didn't want to leave Florida on bad terms with my mom. I gave her a call and told her that I loved her no matter what and I did not want to fight about a townhouse. The next day I left Tallahassee behind, along with everything else. I called a cab and got a ride to the Greyhound Bus Station. I bought a one-way ticket to Atlanta. As I boarded the bus, I was extremely on edge. I was headed into uncharted waters yet another time in my life. I did not know anyone in Atlanta or how to get around. It was a fairly big city and I didn't know what to expect. All I did know was that my life in Florida was over and I was about to enter another length in my journey.

CHAPTER 16
Atlanta Here I Come!!

The ride from Florida to Atlanta was one of the tensest moments I had ever had. So many aspirations ran through my mind as the bus made its way closer to the city I would call home, Atlanta. To many it was a Mecca of sorts. Many people came to this city in search of their dreams. I was one of those people. As the bus rode closer into the city, I could see the skyline forming over the horizon. I had not lived in a city with buildings nearly that tall. Tallahassee's buildings were dwarfed by some of the structures I saw as I drew closer to the city. I made it to the Greyhound Station and took a taxi to a hotel downtown. As I looked around, I embraced everything I saw around me. There was a feeling of being in this state that couldn't explain. It felt like I was home, as if I had a connection to this place. I wanted to stay downtown for the weekend so that I could be around everything and go to the audition. I found a place called the Quality Inn downtown and that was my first stop. I was geared up to take in everything Atlanta had to offer. I was told this city had a well known night life. They had nice restaurants in Atlanta and I wanted to explore everything. I had arrived and was ready to see wait awaited me on my journey to find my place in this big city.

Even though I didn't get the amount of money I really needed, I felt as if I still had a nice amount and I was going to see what Atlanta was all about. I went out the very first night I got there. There were a lot of popular clubs not too far from where I was staying so I decided to go to one of the more popular ones known as Club Visions. I had heard that Diddy owned it. It was right on Peachtree Street, which I would come to learn would be the main street of downtown and maybe even the entire city. I had a lot of fun that night. When I got there, the parking lot was so full. People were just hanging out in the parking lot and it was like a club in itself. The line for the club was one of the longest I'd ever seen. There were hundreds of people there that night. I saw a lot of celebrities in the VIP area. I met a lot of cool people at the club that night. I thought Atlanta was outstanding. Coming from a small town, I wasn't used to a lot of what I was seeing. They say first impressions are the best ones and the city impressed me that night. Little did I know that things aren't always the way they seemed. I'd learn this lesson later on.

The next day I continued my exploration of my new city. I had heard of a place called Underground Atlanta that was supposed to be like a mall that was literally underground. It was a nice place for someone who had never been before. I went shopping for some items for the upcoming audition for *America's Next Top Model*. As I was taking in the sights and sounds of the city, I was pondering a lot about my living situation. I couldn't stay at a hotel forever and didn't want to. I was on limited funds and I'd have to eventually address that situation as well. I also understood that modeling was not going to pay the bills right away if even I succeeded in breaking into the industry. I couldn't worry about that right then though. I had an audition to prepare for.

I woke up that next day full of excitement and anticipation for the tryouts. They were being held at a very well known hotel downtown known as the Westin. I had never done anything on a scale this large. This was the casting for the third cycle of the show. As I approached the hotel, I saw a massive line of girls all there for the same reason I was. I had never seen so many beautiful girls in one place. As I looked around, I could see that many of those girls provided fierce competition. It also seemed like they were looking at me in the same way. It's a well known fact in the world of modeling that the taller women would have a better shot and there were plenty who showed up. In spite of all of this, I was confident in myself and I was really hoping the producers noticed me. Making it on the show would mean so much to me for so many reasons. I felt like I had persevered through a lot and it would give me a chance to tell my story. After waiting in line for hours, I finally had my chance to see the producers. They told us to come in, twenty five girls at once. We all stood in a room and took turns on the microphone telling ours names, age, and where we where from. Unfortunately, I was not picked to go to the next round of selection. I was really upset that I was not picked. I really wanted to be a model and I definitely wanted to go on the show and meet Tyra Banks. I felt like my dreams of modeling had hit a total standstill at that point. It was always a childhood dream of mine to get on television one day and I felt like that was a chance that slipped through my fingers. After the audition, it was back to reality. It was time for me to find a place to live. I couldn't stay in that hotel forever and it was time to move on.

I wasn't quite ready to get an apartment yet because I wasn't employed yet. I knew I had to get a job before I could do that. I had attempted to get an apartment previously and I was told that I had to have verification of employment. Sometimes money alone isn't enough. I looked in the phone book and found an extended stay hotel. I felt like this was a better position for me at the time because I could pay weekly instead of daily. The audition was done and I didn't need to stay down there anymore. My funds were not going to last forever and paying daily for a room along with daily living expenses was not going to work. The extended stay hotel was also near a train station so I had transportation to get around. It was on Piedmont Road, another busy street in Atlanta.

After I got the room, I began to immediately look for a job. I applied at many different places. I tried to find everything from customer service jobs to administrative assistant positions. A few months passed by and I still did not have a job. I had been on quite a few interviews but it was more difficult to find work in Atlanta than I thought. I knew that I had to have a decent job or at least have some decent income coming in so I thought about doing something I hadn't done before. One day I was walking down the street and saw a club called Platinum 21. It had a sign that read "HIRING DANCERS". I contemplated for a while and eventually went inside. The manager came out and told me that he was looking for dancers and that if they wanted to work there, they would have to have a permit. "Anywhere you go in this city, you're gonna have to have a permit baby." he said. I asked him how much it was and he said three hundred and fifty dollars. If I got it, I could work there. He also said that the fee may seem like a lot of money. "Many girls make it back in one night." he said. I surveyed the club and the ladies in there were very pretty. They all had really nice figures. *"I don't have the body type that most of these girls have."* I thought to myself. They were all fairly thick and had big butts that men in the South liked. I was a pretty slim girl and didn't have the body type that they had at all. I didn't believe that I would fit in there. I told him I would think about it and I left. Atlanta was also a city well known for its adult entertainment. There were many clubs like that throughout the city. There was another right down the street from Platinum 21. I decided that I would check that one out also. It was called Tattletales. I went inside and the vibe was very different than the other club. It was predominantly white and there were only a few minorities. It seemed a lot more laid back also. For a beginner, I thought this might be the right place for me to start. I talked to the club manager. It was a woman this time. She was very pretty and after talking to her she said I could work there as long as I had a permit. At this point, I had to go ahead and get the permit even though my funds were running low. I got it the next day and also purchased some dancing shoes and outfits. I was set to start. I was set to work the day shift. My first day was filled with nervousness. I had never done anything like this before. Nevertheless, I knew I had to make some money. To calm myself down, I took a shot of Hennessy. As I got on stage, my heart began to flutter and I just wanted to get it over with. "Now coming to the stage, CHARM!" the DJ announced over the loudspeaker. The music started playing and I noticed men looking at me as I started dancing on the pole. After a little while, some began to come up to the stage and tip me. Even though I was uptight, seeing the money did ease how I felt being up there. Those few minutes seemed like an eternity up there and I was glad when it was over. I was thrilled to get off stage. The lights were beginning to get hot. When I got off stage, men began to ask me for dances on the floor. I made about three hundred dollars that day. I thought I was doing very well. It seemed like it was easy money. Over the course of the next few months, dancing became easier to me. The more I danced, the more comfortable I became with doing it. I also liked the attention I was receiving from the men in the club. I was a very social person and I would just talk to many of them that came through. Many of them were married or divorced or simply needed someone to talk to. I would sit and listen to their problems and just try to be an ear. It wasn't all about dancing for me. Sometimes I would get paid just for listening and giving advice. That was a good feeling because even though the environment was not typical, I was able to help someone and step beyond the level of where we were. I would often hear that I really didn't belong in a place like that and that I didn't seem like that type of girl. I would always reply that I wouldn't be doing this for long and that I had big dreams. As the days and weeks passed by, I continued to work at Tattletales and enjoy the nightlife at regular nightclubs. I was doing whatever I wanted at that point. I felt like I was making money and wasn't worried about much else. I always paid my weekly rent and ensured I had a roof over my head. I had not talked to my mother since leaving Tallahassee. My mind was not thinking about anyone except myself at that time. I was easing back into a destructive path and I was too busy to see it.

In the midst of everything going on, I was lonely. I had met a lot of people in Atlanta although I had not really connected with anyone. That changed one day. I recall seeing an older man, who lived two doors down from me at the hotel, who would always speak to me. He was always respectful. One day he spoke to me and we started talking. "How you doing?!" he asked. "You look like you aren't from around here." he said. I replied "I'm not from around here. I'm from Florida." He seemed very nice and easy to talk to, kind of like a grandfather. His name was Bob and he was from Macon, Georgia. I told him that I had come from Florida to Atlanta to find my family. We became friends from that day forth. Bob also had a truck and it was a blessing to finally know someone in Atlanta with transportation. Atlanta's public transportation definitely had its ups and downs. I really appreciated Bob because he would take me places and I would pay him. I can recall riding one day and he asked me if I went to church. He told me that he did and that he was just trying to live a righteous life. After getting to know Bob, I found out that he had been through a lot in his life. He was a spiritual person and I needed to be around someone like that in my life. He told me that I needed to read my Bible and to always keep my faith in God. I told him that my faith was strong and that I would make sure I read. I began to read more and take my Bible in the club with me every night. Bob also used to have services sometimes and I would go and listen to him. I could tell that Bob was concerned with my lifestyle and where I worked. He never judged me or tried anything. He told me that I needed to get out of the life of dancing because it would lead down the wrong road. I respected him a lot because of that. He would always tell me to be careful out in the streets. I really appreciated his concern. He was genuine. I began to open up to Bob about my life and how I had ended up at this point. Bob asked me one day "Eva, when is the last time you've spoken to your mother? Does she even know where you are right now?" I felt really bad after Bob asked me that. I knew then that it was time to call my mother and check on her.

Even though our relationship had experienced a bit of a strain because of the townhouse incident, I still loved her and I missed her a lot. I called her the next day and we talked for a long time. I let her know that I loved her and that I wanted our relationship to be back to the way it was prior to these events. I looked at her as a sound role model in my life and I needed her in my life as well. I told her that I would call her more frequently. She told me that she loved me and that she just wanted me to be safe more than anything. I felt so much better after talking to mom. Tension between us eased and we became a lot more peaceful after that conversation.

Even though I had finally met a friend in Atlanta, I remained very lonely and missed companionship. Everywhere I went I was usually solo except when I went out with a few girls from the club. There was one club night in particular when I went to Club Primetime with a girl from work named Lisa. We had a lot of drinks that night and I met a guy named Antonio. I was feeling him and I thought he was cute. He told me he was an aspiring rapper. We danced together a lot that night and exchanged numbers. I didn't have a ride home that night because Lisa went home with some guy. Antonio gave me a ride back to the hotel. We began to spend a lot of time together after that night at the club. After a while we started dating. He knew I worked at the club and he was alright with it. It was a different story for me though. It was harder for me to dance in front of other men now knowing I was dating someone. Honestly, the entire lifestyle was starting to take a toll a little. There were many days in which I would wake up around three in the afternoon and go straight to work. I would have to take multiple shots to get through the day because I was getting tired of working in that club. Money in that club began to slow down and I experienced a lot of prejudice actions. I decided I needed to go to a new club to dance. I would need to get yet another permit. I found a club on the west side of Atlanta called Club Babes that didn't require a permit, just a bar fee. I told myself I would go there instead. Maybe I could make some more money there. I had never heard of this club and didn't know what type of environment it was. I didn't have the money for a new permit so I was going either way. I heard that it was on a bad side of town. The street it was located on called Fulton Industrial was notorious for various kinds of illegal activity. I was afraid about going. On the other hand I had to do what I had to do. Club Babes, here I come.

CHAPTER 17
Babes, Drugs, and Thugs

I went inside to check out the club. The whole area was just as everyone had portrayed it to be. You could tell it was a ghetto side of town and that a lot went down in this area. A lot of truckers passed through Fulton Industrial and they frequented the clubs down there. As I walked into the club, it was dim and dark. I noticed that it was bigger than Tattletales. I talked to the manager and he said I could work there as long as I paid a bar fee every time I worked. I started work the next day. I was a lot more nervous working at this club than at Tattletales. You could tell this side of town was bad and so was the club. The entire vibe was not good at all. I remember going back into the dressing room and seeing some girls openly getting high. I just acted like I didn't even see them. I thought to myself *"Eva what in the world have you gotten yourself into now?!"* When I walked out of the dressing room, there were a lot of people in the club. This crowd was much bigger than I was used to. The patrons were also a lot different. There were a lot of dope boys and pool sharks at this club. You could just feel the atmosphere and tell something heavy was always going on. All the dancers looked at me as I passed through. They all had the "Oh there's the new girl" look. I stayed to myself that entire night. I sat at the bar so I could have a drink to calm my nerves. Some guy came up and sat beside me and bought me a drink. He asked me what my name was and I told him I was "Jade". He asked me for a dance and I gave him one. We had a few more drinks and I went and danced for some more people. I made a lot of money that first day and I began to settle in a little. I had even managed a couple of VIP dances. I thought money would come easily at this new club. Little did I know that I only made money because I was the new face on the scene. I was reminded that had a lot to learn. As time passed by, money didn't come as steadily as before. The longer I stayed, the less money I made. The more I was making, the more I was spending so I wasn't saving anything. Many of the girls at that club didn't like me either. There was one dancer I talked to however who I could honestly call my friend. Her name was "Slim" and she always made me feel comfortable when we worked together. Her personality was really lively. She knew that I was the new girl and she befriended me. I had left Tattletales behind and now was working there at Babes full time.

It didn't take for me to become a part of the environment I was in. Seeing these girls openly using cocaine before going out on the floor was strong temptation for me. It brought back memories of the days I had in Florida and the urge for the substance began to creep back into my mind. One day I was in the dressing room and some girls had some. It seemed like everyone, including the DJ, was using some type of drug. I decided to try some cocaine with them and my life went downhill from that day forth. My whole behavior started to change. I was able to stay up a lot later than before. I was high energy all the time. I would come back to the hotel and get high until the sun came up. During this time I would read my Bible and pray that I stopped doing what I was doing. Only then would I go to sleep. Antonio didn't know that I was using and I kept it from him. I didn't want him to look at me like a drug addict. At work, the substance made me feel better to be out there doing what I was doing. I had danced long enough to the point that I understood that all attention from men wasn't good attention and I didn't like their advances all the time. They didn't treat a lot of us ladies with respect. Many of the girls in the club had problems that were deep rooted to their childhoods as well. Some of their stories were compelling. A lot of them said they had either been raped or molested as children. They said they did drugs to ease the pain and repress memories of certain events in their lives. Some would pop pills and use powder at the same time. Dope boys would always hang around the club. They would prey on the girls because they could make money off them, get dances from them, and maybe more. Every day in that club became a party to me. Though it started to get old, I continued to do it. Outside of the club however was a different story. Living at the hotel was starting to take its toll and I wanted to move. Antonio and I decided to move in together. He also didn't want me staying at the hotel anymore. The apartment we found was in Gwinnett County. I was glad to move into a new apartment and out of that hotel. The only drawback was that I lost public transportation because they didn't have buses that ran at decent times. He didn't have a car either so I had to spend money on a taxi to get to the train station to get to work. Making this trek was having an effect financially and physically. I called my mom and told her that I had moved in with my boyfriend. She asked me what my plans were because she already knew that at that point my money from the townhouse was either low or depleted. She assured me that I could call her if I needed anything. She told me she loved me and we hung up.

A few months passed and life living with Antonio started to not be what I thought it would. We began to have problems in our relationship. I found out he started cheating on me while I was at the club. I was upset and I started to give my number away to other guys at that point. I had made up my mind that I liked Antonio but I wanted I do my own thing. I really conceived later on that we rushed into our relationship and didn't take time to get to know each other. I didn't feel peaceful with him yet the relationship continued.

One day I was at the club and that day would change everything. It was a little slow on day shift that day so I was just having some drinks at the bar with a couple girls. This tall gentleman eased his way over to where we were and introduced himself to me. I said hello and he asked me to come over to his table and sit down. I didn't have a problem with it. We went over to his table and I thought he wanted me to dance. He just asked me what I wanted a drink. He was a little different than any guy I had encountered in that club. "What's your name?" he asked. "Jade, what's yours?" I replied. He told me his name was SirTavion and I said that was a very unique name. I had never heard that name before. We sat and talked and I told him I was from Florida and he said he knew a few people from there. He gave me his number and asked me for a few dances. He was cute, though he wasn't really my type. He was tall and slim and I was more into shorter, stockier men. He actually reminded me a lot of the rapper Mos Def. They definitely looked alike.

I did like his vibe though. I definitely danced for him and I could tell he liked it as I was grinding on him. I couldn't talk to him on that level at that time though. I took his number. Still, I never called him. I had so many issues in my relationship and I was talking to other guys. I knew Antonio was talking to other girls. I just didn't want to add on anymore to what I already had going on. It was hard being in a relationship as a dancer. A lot of the girls had boyfriends and I saw half of them tricking off with men in the VIP room. I wasn't one for that. Others were being pimped. It was a crazy world in the club. Many relationships failed because of women doing exactly what they were doing. They would tell me they were "working" but to me that was still viewed as cheating. I didn't need anymore problems than I was already dealing with in my relationship and he just gave me a phone number.

Life continued to be nothing more than a party. It was full of sleep and drugs. The ride back and forth continued. It took me an average of two hours to get to work every day. Life at home with Antonio wasn't good and working at Babes had gotten even worse. The police started to come down on that club because they let girls work there without a permit. There was one day I was working and Slim came running into the club telling everyone that Fulton County Police was outside and they were coming in to check for permits. Many of the girls, including myself, didn't have one. I rushed to the locker room and put my street clothes on immediately. It wasn't worth going to jail over. We all left for a while until they had completed their search. After that day, I had to get my permit because I was afraid to go to jail. It set me back even though I knew I had to. I concluded that one day it would be time for me to look elsewhere. Life at Babes was starting to get worse every single day.

It seemed like work got even worse after I got the permit. Money at the club started to get really slow. Antonio started complaining that I wasn't contributing enough to the bills and that made our relationship even rockier. The club manager noticed how the club was slowing down and he came up with the idea of an industry night in which up and coming rappers could come and perform. This would pull in a much larger crowd as it would become a nightclub and strip club for that one night every week. It was every Saturday night and everyone looked forward to it. All the ladies knew we would make some money. The artists would pay many of the girls to dance while they performed.

That was the only time I worked night shift. I enjoyed industry night because there was a lot of talent in Atlanta and it took the club out of just a strip club atmosphere. A lot of known artists also came to perform on industry night. Even rapper Gucci Mane had his birthday party at the club one night. A lot of the girls got really messed up that night because it was a huge party. I remember that night vividly because I ran into SirTavion. He asked me why I hadn't called him and I told him that I had just been dealing with a lot. "It's all good. I know how it is man." He said. He told me had been dealing with issues of his own and had not been back to the club since we had first met. I believed him because I sure hadn't seen him. He said I looked tired and he asked me if I wanted to go to the VIP and sit down. I said "Yes but I'm honestly trying to make some money. Dances are double in here and I got bills to pay." He just laughed at me and said come on. When we got there, I danced for him and after only a couple of dances he told me "Man, sit down and chill. I know you are on your hustle. I'll make sure you get paid for your time. I just want you to sit down and kick it for a minute." It was then that I realized he was different than any man I had encountered before. He treated me with so much respect. He didn't try to sleep with me or anything. As I sat with him in the VIP, I was drawn to his intelligence. He was very smart. He told me again that I didn't belong in that club dancing. I had heard this from plenty of guys before. I don't know how to explain it but it was different coming from him for some reason. Another thing I observed and liked about him was that he seemed very deep. He had a highly spiritual vibe to him, not like any I'd previously encountered. After being in the VIP room with him, I looked at SirTavion totally different. Time was up in the VIP and he paid me. I was very thankful. I didn't even have to dance that long. I can tell he was just showing love and I appreciated it. He was a really down to earth person. I told him I would definitely call him soon. I went back into the dressing room and changed my outfit because some artists had asked Slim, me, and another girl to dance for them while they performed. We got really high before we went on stage and the artists performed their song "Pool Palace" which would go on to become a regional hit that summer. They came on the platform and the DJ introduced them as BHI. They came with stacks of money that they began to throw all over the stage as we danced. As I climbed up to the top of the pole and flipped upside down and slid, they throw even more money at us. The crowd went wild as we danced and they repeated their chorus over and over. This was all during the beginning of the "making it rain" era in Atlanta. That was my best night at that club. We all left with a box full of dollar bills from just that performance alone. Industry night had somewhat revitalized the club and I was able to make some extra money with so many more people coming in. Girls from other clubs even came to work on Babes' Industry night.

Back at home, my relationship started to decline. Antonio and I were drifting further apart. He was starting to get jealous about me working in the club. He had been there plenty of times and he knew that I was liked by a lot of people that came through. We would have huge arguments because he said I was flirting with other men. I saw him talking to girls at the club plenty of times when he came. I was really tired of the relationship and at that point in my life I really didn't want to be tied down. I had started calling SirTavion more often and talking to him. He went to Georgia State University but he wasn't your typical college guy. His style was different. He was impressive and we got to know a lot about each other. We had a lot in common. I discovered that he had been through a lot of trials in his life as well. I also talked to my mom a lot and told her how much I missed her. She told me that she missed me also. I hadn't seen her since I moved to Atlanta and I was starting to get a bit homesick. She asked me if I wanted to come down to visit and I jumped at the opportunity. A trip out of Atlanta and away from that club for a while would be just what I needed.

CHAPTER 18
Eastside Bound

I was looking forward to my trip to Florida. I missed the Florida air and sun. I told Antonio I would be going to Florida and he was fine with it. He probably had some plans while I was gone anyway. I went to the Greyhound Station and the bus left for Blountstown. As I rode through Georgia, I was pleased to get away. I had gotten a lot deeper into the nightlife in Atlanta than I had planned and stepping away gave me a lot of time to meditate. I arrived in Blountstown and mom was already at the bus station waiting on me. I ran to her and gave her a big hug. We embraced for a long time and finally got into the car. I expressed to her how sorry I was about the whole townhouse event and she said it was ok. Her only concern was for my safety and she just wanted me to be alright. I really wanted to take this time to mend our relationship.

The next day we sat at breakfast and talked. "Eva, what is your transportation situation like up there? I'm sure it's not easy for you to get around." I told her how hard it was and that the transit system was subpar. "Well I don't like the fact that you can't get around. Get dressed because I have a surprise for you." I had no idea what she was talking about. I just went with the flow. We drove to Marianna, about thirty minutes from Blountstown to a car dealership. As we pulled up, I was ecstatic. I couldn't believe I was getting a car. "Ma, I was just coming here to visit. I wasn't expecting you to do this!" She was jubilant to see me so pleased. Mom always had a funny way of showing you she loved you. It was not necessarily the material aspect with her, rather the gesture associated with it. She liked to help people and that was one thing I loved about her. She purchased me an Aqua Blue 2003 Honda Accord straight off the lot. I couldn't believe it. Now I had the ability to see her much easier and I didn't have to ride the bus anymore.

That week I spent in Florida with my mother really helped our relationship. She knew what I had going on and she showed me love regardless. We both had a new understanding of each other after I visited this time. Our relationship started to head back in the right direction. I got a chance to see a lot of old friends while in Blountstown and the week went by quickly. Before I knew it, it was time to head back to Atlanta. I said goodbye to Danielle and she gave me a little money for the ride. "Call me when you make it back ok Eva?" It felt good to hear that she wanted me to call her. I could tell she was worried about me. I assured her that I was fine and that I would be in touch with her. It was time to take the five hour ride back to Atlanta. I didn't mind at all though. I was driving back in my new car.

When I got back to the city, I went straight home to show Antonio. He wasn't there yet so I just settled in and took a bath. I called SirTavion and told him that my mom had got me a car. He was very happy for me. "I can tell you're excited about it!" he said. I told him that I would come see him one day. After a while, Antonio finally came home and I told him my mom had got me a car. I thought he would be upbeat. I was wrong. I actually detected a look of envy on his face. "Oh, so you think you ballin' now huh?" he said. He looked at the car and I could tell he liked it. From that day forth, he'd ask me if he could take me to work so he could ride around in my car all day. The problems began to mount in our relationship. Now that I was mobile, I was constantly being accused of certain things he probably was guilty of. He became very controlling and he started to treat me differently. I stopped letting him drive me to work because I was getting a better feel for the city and no longer needed him to ride me around.

About a month passed and he had done something that finally made me reach a breaking point. My phone had rung and some guy I had met called my phone. I suppose he sensed I was talking to another man and he came over to me and asked who it was. "Who the fuck you talking to Eva? Who the fuck is that?!" I told him it wasn't any of his business and next thing I knew, I was on the floor. Antonio had punched me in my mouth. I couldn't believe it. No man had ever put his hands on me before.

I got up off the floor and he was still yelling and cursing. I packed up all of my belongings I could carry. He saw me packing and tried to become apologetic. The damage was already done. I took everything I had and loaded it into my car. I left immediately. The first person I called was my mom to tell her what happened. I was hysterical. She calmed me down and told me to go stay with a friend until she could figure something out. She warned me not to go back and I assured her that I wouldn't. Later that day, she sent me a thousand dollars and I had actually found a place I could get into. It was meant for me to leave that predicament. I was so glad to have my mom in my life. She really loved me and I appreciated her so much. I stayed with Slim for a few days until my place was available for me to move into. SirTavion would call and check on me from time to time. My new place was on the eastside of town in DeKalb County, much different from Gwinnett. I was happy about the new place and glad to be single. I decided the relationship with Antonio was going to come to an end. There was no way I would stay after something like that. The apartments I moved in were called Kensington Station. Little did I know the area was notorious for all types of criminal activity. It was ok. I needed a place and I planned to stay to myself anyway.

At Babes, the problems there just got worse and worse. I continued doing cocaine with the other girls and drinking and smoking a lot. My mentality was different now because I had more bills. I had my own place and a car to maintain. I couldn't afford to keep these habits up. Tension in the dressing room started to arise also. I had gotten in to some confrontations with one of the girls at the club. One time in particular, I was dancing for a patron and she just came up to me and shouted "Bitch, I'll cut your throat!!" As I looked into her eyes, I can tell that she was high on cocaine and looking for a fight. I was not one to take threats lightly. I thought she was very serious and you never know what someone will do when they are out of their mind. I called SirTavion that night because I was scared. "You need to stop dancing period but for now you need to at least get out of there and find somewhere else temporarily. I understand that you have to pay the bills." The next day, I looked for another club to work in and I found one. It was on the eastside of town and closer to my new place. It was called Pin Ups and it was well known in the city. I thought it would be a little better for me even though I was still dancing. At least my life wasn't being threatened.

The vibe at this club was totally different than Babes. It was much larger and definitely catered to more upscale clientele. There were a lot more businessmen in Pin Ups and they hosted a lot more events and celebrity appearances. I was glad to have a new start yet I did see a few familiar faces from the old club. I came to learn that girls simply went from club to club, and customers did too. When I first started there, I did my usual thing by staying to myself. I was the new face so I made good money when I first started. After a few months, I started to notice that the same dealings that were happening at Club Babes were happening here, just on a different level. Over at Babes, cocaine was the drug of choice. Here at Pin Ups, I noticed the girls liked ecstasy pills. They told me that they made more money when they took them so I began to take some myself. I had rent and all kinds of bills to pay. It wasn't a party for me like it was before. The pills gave me a euphoric feeling and I was friendly toward everyone. I was already social and the pills just made me talk even more. It was easy to talk to guys. I got more men to go to VIP and pay more for dances when I took pills. I didn't see the dangers of taking them so before I knew it; I was doing them more constantly. It began as a weekend thing. It quickly transformed into something I did nightly when I worked. I was spiraling out of control quickly at this club. I was totally out of myself at this point, trying to stay as grounded as I could though it was not working. I felt really lonely sometimes. It had a lot to do with my lifestyle. I never wanted this for myself and one day I would have to change it. In the meantime, I was going hard and didn't care. When I would leave the club, I would buy some cocaine and weed to take home. I would usually go home and call SirTavion when I left work. No matter what time it was, he would always answer the phone and talk to me. I had a feeling my friend knew I was high because he would always say "Ok Eva, It's 'bout time for you to go to sleep sweetheart." I would just say "Ok, I'll call you tomorrow when I get up." That's one thing I grew to love about him. He knew what I did yet he never judged me for it. I really needed a good friend and he was definitely a good friend to me. Over time, my love for him grew and I had a lot of respect and love for him.

Life at Pin Ups went downhill even more as time passed by. I was living a broken record. I had been in these clubs for a couple years at this point. Drugs, dancing, and drinking were my daily routine. Working at the club, standing on six inch heels for hours at a time began to take a toll on my body as well. I was feeling like there was no end to this lifestyle I was living. I understood that it didn't lead anywhere and I grew more desperate to get out of it. I had seen a lot of events since I began dancing at Tattletales. I have seen many girls experience drug overdoses, heard stories of girls I worked with getting killed by pimps or guys they went home with, and women selling their souls just for a few dollars. This wasn't something I wanted to be a part of. As I looked at myself in the mirror at times, I could see how much the lifestyle had worn me down. I was losing weight and dark circles had started to form around my eyes. Yet I continued without thinking about the consequences. I had no idea that they would catch up with me sooner than later. I can recall a night I would never forget. It was September 1, 2005. I remember because it was very close to my birthday. I had a good night at the club and I had made a lot of money. I had popped a pill in the back with some girls so I was rolling. It was something about the pills and music. When I took one, it was as if the music hypnotized me. I could dance for hours. I left the club that night after I had purchased my usual items for the night. I was driving home when a police officer got behind me and began following me. I was extremely paranoid at this point. I had been speeding a little so I turned in to the gas station. I hoped that he would ride on so I laid low at the gas station. After a while I got back in my car and rode only to find the same officer behind me again. At that point, I had a feeling he was going to stop me. Sure enough, he flashed the blue lights and I pulled over. I had marijuana and cocaine in my car and I had a feeling I was going to jail. I began praying. He checked my license and registration. I was worried that he was going to search my vehicle. He just gave me a ticket for having a Florida license and told me to get it taken care of. I was so thankful and relieved. I had dodged a serious bullet and I rode home immediately. If I had never had the drugs in my car, I would not have had to feel that way. I called SirTavion and told him what had happened. He said that the Most High was with me and that it wasn't meant for me to go to jail. "It was a sign Eva." he said. He told me that I had a higher purpose in life and that I needed to change my ways in order to get there. I agreed with him. My life was out of control and I wasn't going to get anywhere I had set out to go by traveling the road I was on. The only thing was that I had gotten myself into a very deep quandary. I was doing too much at one time and everything was moving fast. I hadn't even taken any time to begin looking for my real family since I had been in Georgia. I was trying to get my life under control except it just seemed like one thing happened after the next.

CHAPTER 19
They got me Locked up!

The ticket that I got seemed to loom in the back of my mind every day. SirTavion was concerned and asked me if I had a court date and I told him it was on October 4th. "Are you going?" he asked. "Yeah, I really don't have a choice. If I don't go, I'll have a warrant." I replied. I had never been in trouble with the law before and didn't know what to expect going to court. I figured since it was my first offense I would be ok. I assured him that I would be fine. As days led up to my court date, I continued on my downward routine. My birthday passed and I was now 25 years old and still living a dancer's lifestyle. I wasn't making any progress and everything started to mount up on me. I was missing bills because certain days I simply didn't have the drive to go to the club. It wasn't because of the drugs. It was the fact that I had finally reached my breaking point with dancing. I was tired of it. I knew this lifestyle wasn't for me. Nevertheless my mind was too cloudy for me to figure a way out. The stress of court also mounted. For some reason, I just had a bad feeling about it. It was coming up the next day and I was very irritable. I hated these types of settings. My phone was disconnected so I couldn't call anyone. I was on my own. I said a prayer and prepared for the next day.

I woke up the next day and got ready for the events of the day. The courthouse was actually not very far from where I lived so I just walked. It was only a few blocks away. As I approached, I noticed the line to enter the courthouse was very long. After standing in line for about twenty minutes, I finally made it into the courtroom and it was at full capacity. I sat down and waited for my name to be called. The judge called me to the front and read my charge. She asked me "How do you plead?" she asked. I pled guilty and she asked me if I had the money to pay the ticket that day. I told her I did not and before I knew it, she said that I was in contempt of court. I had no idea what that meant. She then told me to stand over to the left side of the courtroom. There were others who were also standing over on the left side and they had formed a line. Afterward, we were all taken to a different room. My heart was beating a million miles a minute. "*What is going on? Why did I have to come in here and where are we going?*" I had so many questions as I grew jittery with each passing moment. An officer told everyone if we needed to make any phone calls then was the time to do so. I couldn't believe what was going on. I didn't believe it. I called SirTavion. He didn't answer the phone. I left him a message and told him what was going on. I told him I needed some money or I was going to go to jail. I wanted to call my mom although I knew I couldn't. I was so afraid to tell her I was in jail even for a traffic violation and I didn't want to disappoint her. I knew the charge was not very serious and that it wouldn't take much for me to bond out. I came to find out however that I would have to pay a total amount and not a percentage because they added contempt to the charges. My heart sank as I found out how much it would cost. It was almost a thousand dollars and I simply didn't have it. I couldn't come up with the money and therefore I would be going to jail. I tried to call SirTavion once more. My tone of voice was much more serious this time. I couldn't get in touch with him and they took us away to lock up. In the course of a couple hours, I had been searched and booked into DeKalb County Jail. I had reached a new low. How in the world did I possibly end up in DeKalb County Jail for a traffic violation? I was made to exchange my clothes for the county orange jumpsuit. As I looked at the jumpsuit, reality really kicked in that I was now an inmate. After being processed, I was led upstairs to the main section of the jail. The correction officer led me to a cell and ordered the door open. The heavy metal door creaked open accompanied by a loud and eerie echo that reminded you of where you were. There was an older woman already in the cell on the bottom bunk asleep. By this time it was nightfall. I climbed to the top bunk, curled up, and cried streaming tears. I must have awakened the lady because she looked up and asked me if I was okay. "Yes, I've just never been through this before and I'm scared." I managed to say. From that point, I cried and cried until I finally drifted off to sleep, in disbelief at what had happened.

I woke the next day to the sound of all cell doors opening at once. It was about five o'clock that morning. The lady in the cell with me told me it was time for breakfast. I didn't have much of an appetite although I knew I needed to eat. I took one glance at the food on the tray and my stomach slightly turned. The sight of the slimy oatmeal by itself made me not want to eat any of it. I didn't know what was going on and I was just really trying to gather myself. I skipped breakfast and gave it away. By the time the next meal came around, I was very hungry and I had to eat. I didn't have any idea how long I would be in DeKalb County Jail. All I knew was that I absolutely had to change my life. I did not want to ever enter these walls or any others like them ever again.

While I was incarcerated, I learned a lot about life. I had a lot of time to reflect about everything and it didn't take long before I started to. I realized that I had been taking a lot in my life for granted, especially my freedom. I wasn't free in here at all and all inmates were treated like animals. They would place chains on us just like wild beasts and talk to us the same way. I couldn't believe this was going on. I had never been treated so brutally. I had even seen a guard choke a pregnant woman during my time in DeKalb County Jail. That's when I deduced that there was something very wrong about this place. There was a dark, heavy presence over this place and everyone who worked there seemed to flow with it. It was an eerie feeling every single day I was there. I had met a lot of people in a short time and heard their life's stories. It made me turn attention to mine and I realized how blessed I really was.

Another aspect of incarceration that I had to deal with was not having any money. I didn't go to court expecting to go to jail so I didn't have any. I had to come up with a way to get some money. I remembered Eric's phone number and I gave him a call. I told him what I was in for and he couldn't believe it either. He said he would send me what he could and I was thankful. I needed food to eat beyond the rations they gave us.

Two days turned to three and three turned into a week. That first week was hell for me. All I did was sleep a lot and read the Bible. I was really depressed. *"How long would I be in here since I didn't have the money to get out? What was going on with my place and my car?"* I was powerless to answer either question. Being incarcerated was starting to wear on me. I had now been inside that jail for a second week. I finally broke down and called my mom. I didn't want to but I needed her. When I had a chance, I gave her a call. I dialed the number and the phone rang twice. My heart beat faster with each ring. Then I heard her voice on the other end. I immediately broke down and told her I never meant to disappoint her. "What in the world did you do to end up in jail Eva?!" I explained everything to her and how I ended up in this predicament. She listened and I told her how much it would cost for me to get out. Even though I knew she had the money, I honestly didn't want to flat out ask her to get me out. She did not say she was going to get me out either. She told me to take care and that ended the conversation. I sensed that she was trying to teach me a lesson. Deep down, I knew I had gotten myself into this state of being and would have to get myself out of it. I knew then that I would be in jail until my court date, whenever that was.

I was placed in a new cell with a new cell mate. I didn't know exactly how long I'd be in that place so I figured I would get to know her. Her name was Jennifer. She was a heavy set Caucasian female in her mid 20s. As I got to know her, I came to find out the she was only a year younger than me. We started talking and ended up befriending each other while I was there. We had a lot in common. She was also adopted and she had also never met her biological mother. She also had developed some drug addictions. It felt good to talk to someone who identified with what I was going through. It was just a reminder to me that there are many others out there who have a similar story as mine. Going through life feeling misunderstood had always haunted me over the years. I had developed a hard exterior due to so many circumstances I was thrust into. However, underneath was a sweet girl who just wanted to love and be loved. The only thing was that, I really didn't know how because I did not feel like I had received genuine love throughout my life. Jail had made me get back to the inner Eva.

Not being able to communicate with the outside world was agonizing. I was wondering what my family was thinking about. I knew that everyone in Ohio knew about me being in jail. Eric couldn't hold water. I was also thinking about someone else a lot, my friend SirTavion. I know they say that you always think about someone when you go to jail. For me personally, it was just having a clear mind for the first time in a long time. He had always been a good friend to me and always there for me when I needed him. I sat back and reflected on a lot and came to the conclusion that what I needed had been right under my nose the entire time. My love as a friend grew into romantic love and I wanted to be with him. I felt like he was definitely the one for me. It took me being taken out of the club and clearing my mind to realize it. I told Jennifer that I was going to write him and tell him how I felt. I poured my heart out to him in the letter. I was afraid he would have received it was just "jail talk." It wasn't at all. I was very serious. I expressed to him how I felt it was meant for us to be together and that I had fallen in love with him over time and didn't even know it. I also told him I put him on the visitors list. I needed to see him. He had a lot of qualities I liked. SirTavion was such a caring person and very genuine. He was ambitious and had goals and dreams just like I did. He often shared them with me when we had one of our many late night talks. He lived right off of Simpson Road, which is the Westside of Atlanta. He just wanted to make it out of the 'hood. I felt the same way about my life. I too wanted to live a better life and honestly I wanted to do that with him. I sent my letter off and hoped for the best.

During my incarceration, I had experienced so many epiphanies that helped me uncover what I needed to do next in my life. The Most High had shown me so much during this time. I resolved to never dance again nor mess with that hideous substance ever again. I couldn't let Him down. He had taken me and sat me down to clear my head. It was probably the only way that it was going to happen. Every day I grew more and more clear and evermore thankful that He had saved me from the clutches of the darkness. I had found renewed purpose again. No longer was I lost and cloudy. My mind was clear and the message I received was also. Once I got out of here, it was time to resume my ultimate purpose of moving to Georgia. It was time to find my biological family. I was going to give it my all this time.

Three weeks went by and I was remained inside DeKalb County Jail for a traffic violation. The days weren't as rough. Nevertheless, I yearned for my freedom. I was still thinking about my place, my belongings, and the bills that were accumulating. Life outside of these walls continued. One morning, I was lying in my cell and I heard the corrections officer say "Eva Miller, visitor!!" I jumped up. I already had a strong feeling about who it was. No one had come to visit me and I was glad to have someone come in from the outside. I came up the stairs and sat down. It was none other than SirTavion. He had come to see me and I couldn't have been happier. As I picked up the phone, my spirit lifted a bit. I looked at him through the glass window and wished that glass shield wasn't there. He looked like he did too. "Got your letter." He said and cracked a smile. That made me laugh and we started talking from there. "It's crazy to see you in here man. I'll be glad when you get out." He said. "Who are you telling?!" I said to him. "Well, I have contemplated a lot on this letter you sent. I appreciate it but honestly I need to know if this is this serious or just how you feel because of where you are?" I can understand why he asked. I had never told him anything like this before. "Yes Tay. You really don't understand. I'll be able to tell you more and show you when I get out of here." We talked about so many different topics and I told him I couldn't wait to get out. We said that when I did that we would definitely hook up. Before we knew it, our conversation was cut short and time was up. It went by so fast. I was glad that we got a chance to talk about a lot. I told him I would see him soon and he left. I went back to my cell and laid down, feeling better than any time I had been there. That was one of my best days in there.

The next morning I was awakened to my name being called again. I wasn't expecting anymore visitors. They told me that I was going to court. I jumped for joy because I knew I was probably leaving. They chained every up as usual when we walked to court. As we walked chained in a straight line, I was anticipating going to the courtroom. Once we made it, they divided men on one side and women on another. There was a different judge this time. He called me to the front and asked me what I plead. I told him guilty again. As he looked at my charge he asked "Ms. Miller, how long have you been incarcerated?" "Six weeks, your honor." I replied. He looked shocked and said "Time served." The tone of his voice suggested that I should not have been there as long as I was. Internally I could have won the gold medal in gymnastics. I felt like jumping up and down. I kept my composure though. I went back to my cell, gathered everything I had, and they released me. I was finally free once again. I left that dark building with a new view on life. I didn't take anything for granted and now it was time to get my life together.

CHAPTER 20
Finding True Love

The first thing I did was run home immediately. It had been six weeks and I was afraid that they may have evicted me from my place. As I approached, I saw a letter on the door and the blinds were open. I saw then what had happened and my heart sank. I had been evicted and not even a remnant of my things remained. No clothes, no furniture, and most importantly no pictures. Everything Eva had given me to help me on my path was gone, with all the things I had in my car as an exception. Aside from my memories, I was back to square one. I didn't have anywhere to go. All I had was fifteen dollars, my purse, and my car keys. The sun was beginning to set and I couldn't stay out there. I didn't have a cell phone so I couldn't call SirTavion. I was thankful to still have my car intact and I sat inside and contemplated my next move. The car didn't have any gas so I couldn't drive it anywhere. I decided to go downtown to a shelter and sleep for the night. Sleeping inside a shelter that night reminded me of being in jail. The atmosphere was similar. The main difference was that you could leave. I felt really bad. I had really hit rock bottom at this point. I woke up the next day, took a shower and left quickly. You couldn't stay too long that next morning and everyone had to leave by a certain time. I walked downtown for a while and I eventually got in contact with SirTavion. I called him and told him I was out and that I was catching the train to his house. I was so happy to see him and it felt really good to be around him. We had a lot of fun and he helped ease the stress of what I was going through.

We talked about how we wanted to be together and how funny it was that we were even talking about this. He and I shared true friendship. Who had an idea it would transform into true love.

I called my mom and told her that I was out of jail. I told her that I had lost my place though I still had my car. "Well, you need to sell it to get some money Eva." She said. I understood I would have to do something on my own. I wasn't going back to the club to dance ever again. I knew that I could go back to Florida if I wanted to. I had to do this on my own though. It was time for me to stand up and be the woman I knew I was. SirTavion and I went through all the numbers we had, asking everyone if they knew anyone who was trying to buy a car. Thankfully we found someone. He said that he was looking for one for his daughter. We set up a meeting for the next day at the car and I spent the night with SirTavion that night. The next day, I ended up selling the car. I needed it because I was down to two bucks. I couldn't drive it because it had a flat tire that I didn't have the money to replace when I got out. The gentleman replaced it. I signed over the title and that ended the transaction. I was thankful for the blessing. I now had a little money. At this point, I had to figure out my next move.

I stayed with SirTavion for about a week while I figured out what I wanted to do. One thing I knew was that I needed to get out of Atlanta for a while. I knew that the temptations were still fresh and easily accessible so it was best for me to totally remove myself from that environment. I needed to go somewhere that had a little slower pace. I decided to call Wanda and see if I could come back to her place for a little while. Things were different and Wanda had her own place. She said she was fine with it and to just let her know when I would be coming. I was trying to turn my life around and the last thing I needed was to backslide. I was alright with going back to Hamilton. I remember a lot of good people there. I told SirTavion that I had decided to go back to Hamilton. He was sad yet he understood and also thought that it was best for me to leave. He just wanted to see me get my life together and that it wasn't going to happen in Atlanta. After all, he was trying to finish up his last year of college and had his share of adversities going on as well. This was an individual journey I had to take. In order to be with him the way I wanted to, I knew that I had to make a full transformation from what I had been doing. We spent a few more days together and I loved every minute of it. It felt good to be with someone who understood me and treated me the way he did. For once in my life, I felt true love. I was sad to leave him yet I left knowing it was for the greater good. We would meet up again. For now it was time to part ways.

I arrived back to Hamilton to a place that no longer resembled the Hamilton, Ohio I remembered. I hadn't been back in a few years. I would visit every now and then when I lived in Florida but it had been quite some time. There was a feeling of dreariness at every turn. Previously vibrant areas no longer existed and even some of the people I knew had changed. As I walked around the city, I couldn't believe the state of some of the landscape. Many places that once served as homes for families were now nothing more than vacant lots. Other buildings were shells of their former selves. I noticed a lot of aspects about Charles had changed too. Something just didn't seem right. It seemed as if everyone else was oblivious to it. Personally, I could see a difference because it had been a long time since I had been there and seen him. He had a hint of insanity underneath his outward persona. Even though he had his ways, I viewed him as a warm hearted man as a child. Now, he had evolved into something different, much more cold and calculated. I believe he carried resentment because I didn't speak to him nearly as often as I did before I found out he was not my real father. I didn't know how long I would be in Hamilton. As always, I would try to make the best of it.

The days in Hamilton went by fast. It was wintertime and I was always over Tone's house. He also lived in Hamilton after all these years and I was glad to have a good friend from childhood still there. I didn't enjoy it over Wanda's house at all. She only had a one bedroom apartment and I slept in the living room on the couch. I was thankful for a place to lay my head but I didn't want to be in the way. I had a perception of that place that no one else did or else turned a blind eye to and I tried to stay away as long as I could every day. I knew Charles would be there and I really didn't have much to say to him. A few months passed by and I was starting to settle in again.

One night after I had gone out, I came back in to find Charles lying on the floor asleep. I changed into my night clothes and laid on the couch. I was tense yet eventually drifted to sleep. Later that night, I was awakened with a chilling feeling. It was as if I was being watched in the dark. I opened one eye and tried my best to discern what was happening. As moonlight filled the room, I noticed that Charles was closer to the couch than he was before. He had the covers over himself and I could tell he was awake. I noticed his hands going in an up and down motion. I asked myself "*Is this man looking at me and touching himself?*" I tried to act like I was asleep as I laid there weary of him. I turned to make him assume I was waking up and then I went to the bathroom. I had a sick feeling in the pit of my stomach. I couldn't believe what I saw. It was dark in the room. Still, I was not stupid. To this day, I don't believe he knows I saw him. I guess he does now. That night changed everything. It took the last ounce of dignity I had for him away. I now viewed him as a sick individual who had some mental problems. I pray to this day that he finds help.

The next morning I called SirTavion and told him what happened. I had to tell someone. I knew I couldn't tell Wanda. She adored Charles and probably wouldn't have believed me. When he answered the phone I just broke down. I told him everything and he was very upset. He told me that I wouldn't have to stay there and that he would send for me to come back to Atlanta. It was like I was not able to find peace at all. I left Atlanta to get away from crazy situations and went right back into some. I wasn't even in Hamilton six full months and it was time for me to go. I felt like everything happened for a reason and perhaps my reason for coming back was so that I could observe what I had never noticed before. I went over Tone's house and told him what happened. He thought it was also disgusting and was glad that I was leaving. He was always in and out of Atlanta so I'd see him. I was going back to be with SirTavion. Therefore I was certain it would be different when I went back to Atlanta this time. I wouldn't be dealing with so much temptation and I would have someone in my corner to keep me on the right track. SirTavion told me that he would send for me in a few days and to just take time out to gather my stuff for the rest of my time there. It was time to leave Hamilton for the last time. I wouldn't live there anymore. Tone took me to the Greyhound Station a few days later and I was Atlanta bound. Hamilton had changed, along with many people in it. I would miss a few people I had reconnected with. We would be in touch. I was anticipating my return to Atlanta to start a new chapter in my life, this time with my man SirTavion.

When I arrived in Atlanta, it was a totally different feeling than when I had come in from Tallahassee a few years back. I was now much wiser and more focused. I had become even more spiritual and I had faith that God would eventually work things out for me this time around. I wasn't the same person I was before. I didn't intend on going back to who I was. I had too many aspirations ahead of me. He truly gave me another chance and I would not take it for granted.

SirTavion was in his last semester of school and so we lived at his mother's house until his graduation. Two months later, my man graduated from Georgia State University. It was so good to see him make it. He had been through his own share of trials and tribulations and he never broke. He was a strong brother and that was one thing I loved about him. He had a backbone. Seeing him graduate with the Class of 2006 was an inspiration to me. Observing him accomplishing his goals served as strong motivation for me and my own. Eventually after he graduated he was blessed to find a job in his field and we moved into our own place together. It was now the end of the year and I was finally more stable. I really began to miss my mom. Later that month around Christmas, we took a trip down to Florida to see her. I hadn't seen her since she purchased the car for me when I was with Antonio. SirTavion and I were both looking forward to it. He wanted to get out of the city for a little while himself.

We rode the Greyhound to Florida. After a grueling trip, we made it to Blountstown. Wade picked us up and took us to mom's house. As soon as I saw her, I dropped everything and gave her a big hug and kiss. I was overjoyed to see her. It felt remarkable to be home and to have SirTavion there with me was just the icing on the cake. Mom told me that I looked really good and that I had put on a few pounds. Then she glanced over at SirTavion as to call him out as the culprit. I was having a nice, peaceful time. That all changed in an instant as I saw Janet, Charles' sister show up. "Eva Danielle Hammond" was the first thing she said to me. She was already trying to start trouble. I didn't feed into it because I knew her provocateur nature already. I paid her no attention. I was just glad to be home. Though the energy in the house changed a bit, I made the best of the trip. I tried to spend as much time with my mom as I possibly could. It was hard because there was always someone in her face all the time. Tina was also at the house all the time. Between her and Janet, I don't know who was in my mom's face the most. At one point, I finally got a chance to talk to her alone. She revealed to me that she had been sick and that she was waiting on some test results to come back from the doctor. My mom never revealed what type of tests however she did at least keep me in the loop of what was going on. I appreciated that and she probably didn't want me to worry.

Over the course of our trip, I got a chance to show SirTavion where I used to hang out and he met some of the people there. After a few days, it was time to get back to Atlanta. We enjoyed our trip. The only bad thing was the revelation my mother had shared with me. Though I tried not to worry, she stayed in the back of my mind from that point on.

CHAPTER 21
Blood is Thicker Than Water

Life in Atlanta was starting to take off. It felt so good for me to be back in my own place again. Even more so, I was thankful to have peace and clarity. I was also grateful to have SirTavion. We worked well together and home life was going really well, until one fateful day. I had gotten a call from my mother. "Well Eva, the test results came back from the doctor." I was nervous about what mom was going to say next. She informed me that they detected cancerous cells in her throat. "No! Are you serious?!" I said to her. It made me recollect for a moment. Mom did smoke a lot of cigarettes over the years. I broke down immediately and told her that everything was going to be okay. My heart hurt badly for her. I told her that I would pray for her and that I loved her very much. She asked me not to say anything to Wade because she had not told him yet and wanted to tell him when she felt the time was right. I respected her wishes and from that day forth, I talked to her all the time.

About a month passed and mom called me saying she had a surprise for me. She told me that she bought me a car. "You need to have transportation to come visit me every now and then." Mom said. I gathered what she really meant underneath. She wanted me to have a vehicle so that I could come back to check on her more easily and more often. I was so thankful for that blessing. We needed a car very badly and I was glad that I would be able to go see her much easier now that she was sick. All I had to do was get to Florida and pick it up. Wade came from Florida with one of his many lady friends, picked me up, and took me back to Tallahassee. That was where mom had moved so she could be closer to work and the doctor's office for chemotherapy. She owned a few townhouses in the city so she simply moved into one. When I got there, I went and sat near here immediately. Tina was there as well. She was always around, sometimes too much to me. Mom always told me that she was there to help her. To me something about Tina just never felt right. Natalie had said the same thing when she was living with us. I always recollected how she came out of nowhere once my grandmother passed. I just wanted my mother to know that I was there for her and that I was right by her side. We talked about the past and laughed at old memories. I was glad to spend some time with her. I could tell that she was getting sicker. I was happy to see her spirits were still up. The next day I went and got the car and I was so joyous. It was silver, which was one of my favorite colors. I went straight back to my mom's house to thank her for the kind gesture. I had sold my car that last year and now I had another. She was just glad to see me happy. My mom was that type of person. Danielle always got joy from doing for others even though some people would try to take advantage of her kindness. I stayed for a week before heading back to Atlanta. Honestly I didn't want to leave her. She had her husband, Wade, and Tina helping her out so I figured she would be alright.

A few months passed by and everything with her health was pretty stable until I got a call from Wade one day saying she was in the hospital. I was shocked to hear this news and I didn't take it very well. I got off the phone with him and called the hospital immediately to speak to her. Once I finally got through, she said she was ok. "Ma, I'm driving down there to see you!" I told her. "It's alright Eva; I'll be released in a day or two." She reassured me. She got out and felt well for a while. SirTavion and I drove down to see her that next weekend to spend some time with her. We grew closer than we ever had been. I really loved her and she loved me. I was glad we had patched up our relationship and that we had began bonding on an entirely different level. However, this was a short-lived experience. On May 29, 2007 I got a call that would alter my life permanently. Charles, of all people, called me. "Eva, did you hear?" he asked. "Hear what?!" I replied. I knew Charles wouldn't be calling me if it wasn't something serious. "Danielle passed." He told me. "What?!" I asked. I honestly didn't believe him. After I heard this, I was hysterical. I dropped the phone. It was as if my legs gave out from under me when he told me that she was gone. I felt utter devastation upon hearing this news. There was pain on two fronts. One she was gone and two I had to hear it from the same man who took me away from her in the first place. My entire world had been turned upside down. After I hung up with Charles, I was in a dream state. This just couldn't be real. There was no way my mom was gone from my life when we had just started bonding again. I had never lost anyone this close to me in my life and it was absolutely lamentable. I called SirTavion and told him what had happened and he was sad immediately. He had really grown to love my mom as they spent time together. They even talked when I wasn't around. A little later, Wade called and told me the news. He didn't know that I already had knowledge that she was gone. "Do you need me to come down and help with the funeral arrangements?" I asked. "No that's alright. I'll take care of everything myself. There's no need for you to rush down here." He replied. Who was he kidding? My mother had just passed away and I needed to be there as soon as possible. The next day, I packed up some items and headed to Florida. It was a sad and somber drive for me and I cried much of the way. It was hard for me to focus because my mother was the only thing on my mind. I didn't know what I was going to encounter when I got to Florida. So many thoughts sifted through my mind. I called Wynette and told her what had happened. She told me that she was coming to Florida to support me. I was glad because SirTavion couldn't get off from work and he wasn't able to come.

After a six hour drive, I finally made it to Tallahassee. I went to the townhouse mom was living in and Wade was there. I gave him a hug and we talked for a few minutes. He was really brief with me and had an air about him that I hadn't seen before. It was then that I saw that everyone from North Carolina had come also but granny was the only one at the hospital when my mother passed. As I came inside, I noticed that they were all very cold toward me. I felt like they revealing their true selves now that my mother had passed away. I felt so alone and depressed. Wade had his family there to support him and I was grieving alone. I was so happy when Wynette made it to town. Everything had been all about Wade and no one seemed to be worried about my well being. I was grieving just as much if not more. Accepting her death was a giant pill to swallow in itself. I wished I could have been there for her last moments. I really did.

As I tried to get through this, I began looking for mementos to remember my mother by. There were some African statues that she had that we both loved and would talk about. I decided that when it was all done that I would take some of them back to Atlanta with me. The funeral was in a couple of days and I was just trying to keep myself together. This funeral was going to be one of the hardest moments of my life. I was going to read a piece that SirTavion and I put together. I wanted to send my mother off with love and dignity. The days passed quickly and before I knew it, it was time to bury my mother. I prayed for the Most High to give me strength.

I woke up that morning with a sadness that cut deeper than any I had ever felt. That night before, I didn't sleep very much because of so much anxiety. All I could fathom was the fact that I was going to be seeing my mother for the last time. Wynette and I got dressed that morning and left Tallahassee for Blountstown. Everyone was meeting at the house there. When we arrived, everyone else had already arrived. Charles and Eric had made it down for the funeral. I hugged Eric and lined up with everyone. We all drove over to the church and lined up outside as we prepared to view her body one last time. As we approached her, my heart was pulsating rapidly. Just the thought of seeing her lying there lifelessly was tragic to me. I made it to the casket and saw her laying there as if she was asleep although I knew that she wouldn't be waking up from this. She looked very natural and like herself. As soon as I saw her, tears began rushing from my eyes uncontrollably. This was a pain that I cannot explain to you all. Anyone who has lost a parent knows what I mean, and until you do you honestly cannot possibly understand. I was overwhelmed and praying earlier had kept me together. I gave her a kiss on her cheek and I sat down to try to collect myself. After everyone got a chance to view her, they came and closed the casket. It was at that very moment when it hit me that I would never see her again. I wanted to break down so bad. On the other hand, deep inside I knew that I had to be strong. I had to send my mother off in my way and I couldn't have my mind in disarray. It was time to read my poem to her. Before ascending the stairs, I stood for a brief moment and gazed at the snow white and gold casket that would be my mother's final bed. I got up to the podium and let my heart speak:

JEWELS OF THE EARTH
SOME JEWELS IN THIS WORLD ARENT NECESSARILY
STONES
BUT THEY GLOW FROM WITHIN WITH A PRESENCE SO
STRONG
LIKE THE SUN, THEY BRING WARMTH AND JOY TO SO
MUCH
THEIR ENERGY IS LIKE SUNRAYS TO THE LIVES THAT
THEY TOUCH
PRICELESS ARE THE MEMORIES THESE JEWELS CAN
CONCIEVE
ALL IT TAKES IS REFLECTION AND THEY'RE NOT HARD
TO RETRIEVE
BEING SO PRECIOUS TO SO MANY IS AN HONOR IN
ITSELF
LETS NOT FORGET THIS SHINING JEWEL AS LONG AS WE
HAVE BREATH
SOME JEWELS ARE UNFORGETTABLE, THEIR STORIES
ARE GREAT TO TELL
WE'LL ALWAYS LOVE OUR JEWEL OF THE EARTH, HER
NAME WAS DANIELLE

I could tell that the piece had touched some people, especially her co workers. It made me feel good because that was all I wanted to do. I wanted to send her off with some kinds words and always let her know how much I loved her. The funeral lasted just a bit longer and it was time to go to the graveyard. We buried her Saturday June 2nd, right next to her mother Eva. Shortly after, we talked to a few people and Wynette and I headed back to Tallahassee. I was wiped out both mentally and physically. I hadn't slept much the night before and I was fatigued. I knew that now that Danielle was gone, things were going to be a lot different. Wade and I would have to stick together more now because mom was gone.

When I woke up from my nap, Wade and his family from North Carolina had made it back to Tallahassee. As I came downstairs, the entire house fell silent and the vibe was not good. It was a weird feeling. It felt really frigid around them. I tried to be as pleasant as possible, for my mom's sake. The next day, Wynette left to go home and I went back to feeling alone. Wynette hadn't been gone two hours before everything flipped. Once she left, Wade and his family went out for breakfast without me. When they came back, I was downstairs sitting on the couch. Honestly, my mind was gone at this point. I was out to lunch. I thought about the funeral and how my mother was no longer around. That house felt so empty to me without her presence. As they came in, they all sat down around me and I started to feel uncomfortable. It was like wolves circling prey. Wade stood up in front of the TV and handed me a piece of paper and said "Mom signed this a day before she died." I was shocked because I didn't even know what it was or what was really going on. I took a look at the paper and read it. It was a copy of a new will that had been drawn up right before she died. It was dated that she had signed it on the very day before she passed away. I found this to be very weird because mom had recently told me herself that she had a will already in place if something was to happen to her. I read the "new will" and it stated that everything goes to Wade from car to properties, Janet, Charles' sister was included to receive some money, Verne's daughter was to receive some jewelry, and even Tina was left one of my mom's houses. Her husband also received a property. As I read this "new" document, there was nothing bequeathed to me in the will. Everyone sat and watched me as I scrolled through the document. After I was done, I gave it back to him and continued to watch TV. I thought to myself *"Did I really and truly see what I thought I did? If so, is Wade was really trying to do what I think he is?"* I told Wade if he wanted to speak to me, to please do so in private. "Let's go upstairs." I told him. I felt like he was very disrespectful for that. He was putting family business right out in front of them and he was also trying to call me out in front of his family. Wade knew they really didn't care for me, especially now that my mom was gone. We went upstairs and he did most of the talking. I merely sat back and listened. I was seeing a side of him that I had never seen before. Mom had passed and he was doing a complete 180. He told me if I need anything that I would have to come through him. He spoke to me as if he was some sort of royalty and I was some sort of peasant. I didn't like this vibe he was emitting. The more he talked, the icier his eyes grew. He resembled his father more than ever before and I saw flashes of Charles as he spoke. I had never seen him look at me so cold. What did I possibly do to him? I always treated Wade with love and didn't understand where this animosity was coming from, until he kept running his mouth. "I was so jealous of your relationship with ma. She loved you SO much!" he snarled at me. "I just don't understand how she still loved you after all you did. How could she still love you after that? I couldn't stand that!" he went on to say "You think you're getting half don't you?" Then he said again that if I needed anything that I would now have to come through him to get it. "I don't need to go through you! If I need anything, I'll go through God!" I told him. I wasn't about to bow down to this sucker of a man. The truth had finally come out after all these years. He had been housing this for a very long time and it had finally come out in one volcanic eruption. I never looked at him the same after that moment. It was very cutting on so many levels and really confirmed to me what he was attempting to do. He despised me and wanted to selfishly rub me out of my mother's will. He never really loved me as his sister. He only dealt with me because he knew his mother loved me unconditionally. Though it was very hurtful, it gave me valuable insight. It served as a major life lesson for me. Money often destroys families. I had heard about it plenty of times. Honestly, that showed me where everyone's mind was as far as my mother's affairs were concerned. I was grieving and dealing with the pain of losing her and here he was talking about wills and money.

Seeing Wade turn like this was very sad indeed. I already didn't have his mother anymore and now he had shown his true colors. "When are you leaving?" he demanded to know. The way he asked plainly had undertones that I was no longer welcome there. "And by the way, those statues you have? They need to come back to me." I couldn't believe it. He was being spiteful at this point. He knew how mom and I loved those statues. On top of this, he was already receiving everything according to this "new will". He only wanted them back because I wanted them. I thought to myself "*I'm not giving you anything back. You can't take these away from me because you're being hateful.*" I was going to leave the next day and get back to Atlanta to someone I knew loved me genuinely. I had no one except SirTavion at this point. I didn't know where my real family was. I was out here alone again. Wade had shown his true colors after all these years and most of his family never liked me in the first place. They knew I wasn't Charles' daughter and that's why they treated me that way. Mom was gone and all I had was the Most High. The aftermath of Danielle's death affected my life on a number of levels and it was time for me to get back home so I could collect myself and mourn for her privately.

CHAPTER 22
It's Eva's time to Shine

The next day, I left Tallahassee without speaking to any of them. Why should I? They didn't want me around and their actions showed me. I now saw them for what they were and it confirmed for me the old saying that blood is thicker than water. I was so happy to get back to Atlanta and SirTavion. I missed him so much and I knew he would be there for me. I was glad to have him in my life because I had a feeling that some days for me following her death would very trying times for me. I would have to stop myself from sinking into a depression. I yearned for my real family more than ever before. I was on an island of despair all alone. Each day went by with me thinking about Danielle, how Wade and his family treated me, and how much I needed to find my real family. I prayed everyday for God to take this pain away from me and some days were better than others. SirTavion tried to do the best he could to be there for me. He expressed to me that he understood that he could only do so much. One day he told me that he was going to get me a puppy. He actually did. I was very surprised. It was a female Jack Russell terrier and her name was Queen. She was black and white and had a constant motor. She was extremely energetic and kept me very active. I loved that dog. She really did help me out so much during my time of grieving. She now has a new owner. I am thankful that she served her purpose for me. I grieved a lot and without any familial support, it was very hard. I really felt lost and I needed them in my life, especially after what happened in Florida.

Over time, the Most High turned these feelings into a positive for me. It gave me the drive to want to find my relatives. I drew on all the information I gained from Eva and from certain documents I had. All I could do is start putting the pieces together and start a trail.

I told myself that I was going to find them no matter what. My determination was at an all time high. After finding out what I knew from Eva, I had tried to search for my mother afterward. The birth certificate identified her as Jeannie Beaver although her signature was Jeannie Hammond. That is all I knew. It did not have her birth date, only the state she was born in and her age. This is why my search brought me to Georgia in the first place. I searched her name time and time again with both combinations and got no results. Something told me that I would have to take a different approach.

I had never tried to find my sister before. I knew her name was Iesha so I started to search her name in various databases. One night, I was on MySpace and decided to try theirs. I was hoping that she probably lived in California. That would help me narrow the search. All of the names popped up for the State of California. I sat down that night and sent a friend request to each and every Iesha in the state. I was up late into the night. It ended up being a total of well over six hundred names and I had contacted them all. I was really tired and finally got some rest. I felt good about the search and I prayed that it would yield the results I'd been seeking my entire life.

It was summertime and I had started to feel a little better. It was a summer that would never forget. I can recall it plain as day, more specifically July 10th, 2007. It was a regular nice evening at home. SirTavion was off and we were just talking. "Have you checked your MySpace page today?" he asked. I had not since earlier that day so I decided to. I had a message from one of the women I had contacted. She asked me if I knew her. I replied to her and said "No, I don't. I'm just looking for my sister." She replied saying that she had a sister that was a year younger than her and that her birthday was in September. I started to get butterflies in my stomach like never before. It was very surreal to me that this was so coincidental. She also asked me where I've lived. I told her that I was born in Los Angeles and that my birthday was September 18th and that my mother's name is Jeannie Hammond. I couldn't believe what was going on. In my mind, I was somewhat scared because I knew this was something I had searching for my entire life. To be on the cusp of what could quite possibly be me finding my big sister was overwhelming. I was afraid that it wasn't going to be her. I had never been this close before and all I could do was what I had been doing all along, praying. I got another inbox message from her and my entire life changed from that moment forth. It simply said "Yep, you are my sister. This is so CRAZY and you have a younger brother. His name is Kevin Hammond." I dropped down to the ground and starting immediately thanking the Most High. I was crying rivers of joy unknown. For the first time in my life, these were tears of joy and happiness. I couldn't believe it. I really couldn't. I laid right there on the floor and didn't move. I just wept and wept. Not only did I have a sister, I had a brother also. SirTavion came in and initially he thought something was wrong with me. All I could do at that point was point at the computer. His mouth dropped to the floor. I always wonder what was going through his head as he read that message. I was so thankful beyond measure. God had blessed me with something I had been yearning for my entire life, my family. My dream had come true. This hole that I had in my heart for years could finally be filled. Jeannie and I would finally be reunited after more than two decades and I couldn't wait to talk to her. This was the best moment of my life at this point. It was like a heavy burden was lifted off my shoulders instantly and I felt peace inside that I had never felt before. She gave me her phone number and after I collected myself I gave her a call.

There were so many questions I had and wanted to ask her about the family. As she answered, I was extremely tense. The first time I heard her say hello, I knew my sister was a California girl. It felt indescribable to actually hear her voice. I had called a family member for the first time. Iesha was and always will be the first person from my family that I ever spoke to. "How are you?" I asked her. She told me that she was doing great and she was also in disbelief that we were actually talking. The first question I had was about our mom. I wanted to know where she was. "Where's mom?" I asked with anticipation. "Well, she died." Iesha told me that Jeannie had passed away in 2001. It took me right back to reality. I was crushed to here this. Finding my family became bittersweet upon hearing this news. I started crying again and told her how hurt I was. It was hard for me to talk to her after hearing this news, not because I didn't want to. It was only because I knew I would never see Jeannie face to face. "I just lost my adoptive mother last month!" I told my sister. I could tell she felt compassion for me. "I'm sorry to hear that. Well, just know that you have a big family. You have two aunts and lots of cousins." She told me. I asked her about my brother and she said he was a friend on her MySpace page. I found him and asked for a friend request. As I looked at my brother, I could tell we were related. He looked a darker male version of me. SirTavion looked at him and said "Man, there's no denying it! You two are definitely brother and sister." He pointed out quite a few features that were similar to mine. My brother answered my request and sent me a message. The first message he sent me he said "You look just like mom!" and he sent me a picture of Jeannie. I will always love him for because that was the first time I had ever seen a picture of her. He had shown me what my mother looked like. I had wondered for so many years about this. I cried as I looked upon it for the first time. I saw myself in this woman. I looked in the mirror and for the first time in my life I knew who I resembled. Kevin and I exchanged numbers and I gave him a call as well. We had an instant connection and a great conversation. I was hoping he would accept me. I found out a lot about my mother Jeannie from Kevin. He said that she was a good person who had a good heart. He painted a good picture of our mother and I was glad to get some insight into who she was directly from one of her children. However, as with so many others moments in my life, there are always disruptions. After about a week, I called my brother to see how he was doing. "Hello." he said. "Hey Kevin. How are you doing?" I asked. Next thing I knew, he passed the phone and his voice was replaced by a woman's voice. "Hello?" I said. "Hi Eva, this is your aunt. I just want to say that this is a lot for Kevin and Iesha to handle right now." "I mean, we do not even know who you really are. A lot of people can play games over the computer and I think you're coming on a bit too strong." I was taken back. I couldn't believe this woman told me that. After all these years of searching, she had the nerve to say that it could be a joke. "*Who has time to play such a sadistic joke?*" I angrily thought to myself. "I just found Iesha last week. I lost my adoptive mother not even two months ago and I do not have anyone." I told her. "Well, I'm sorry to hear that but we cannot be there for you." She coldly replied. I was very offended and I decided to get off the phone with her before I said something disrespectful to her. I came to find during that conversation with my aunt that I also had an uncle. His name was Sidney. My uncle had also passed. At least she told me that much about my family history. What was I to do now? I had found my family after all these years only to be met with an uneasy reception. She made me feel as if I did something wrong. I was given the impression that I had disturbed their lives with my presence. I couldn't even talk to my brother and sister. Not to mention, my adoptive brother didn't want anything to do with me. I thought about both of my mothers and said to myself *"If either of them were alive right now, things would be totally different."*

I was now grieving for two mothers at once and many of those days were extremely difficult to deal with. Many people would probably ask me how I can grieve for someone I really did not know. My reply would be that she is my biological mother and therefore we are always connected. We'll always have a mother/daughter bond. I have always loved Jeannie even though I didn't know her. That will never change.

I sank into a bit of a depressive state over the next few weeks following my talk with my sister. I looked back on the events that had recently transpired. The first conversations with my siblings went well. The turning point was when I tried to call my sister and brother back. I really couldn't believe it. I had found my family after twenty six years and now I couldn't even get to know them. My aunt claimed that it was lot for them, yet what about me? She had no idea of my background or what I had been through. To say that it was too much for them did not sit well with me. I had no one and my own family didn't want to be there for me. I was starting to gather that finding my family may not be quite how I envisioned it to be. I knew I had to get back to my life even though I was dealing with so much turmoil inside. I didn't know what I wanted to do.

I didn't like the feelings I was dealing with and I knew I had get myself out of this slump. At some point, one has to move forward. I was reaching this point in my healing process. One day SirTavion and I were watching the local news and they said that *American Idol* was coming to Atlanta for auditions for the upcoming seventh season. I had done some singing in the past so I figured I would go try out. I needed to do something fun to lift my spirit. I only wanted to go have fun, meet some eccentric people, and possibly even get on TV. That next week, I went down to the Georgia Dome and registered for the auditions. They would be the next day and I was very anxious. I had something new to look forward to.

I woke up the next day around 4:30 in the morning. I had to get down to the Georgia Dome early because the line was going to be a mile long. SirTavion came with me for support. We decided to take the train because it was the easiest way to get there. No sooner than we entered the station, we were met with an array of voices from many people singing. "What are all these people doing so amped up this early? It's not even six o'clock yet." SirTavion said. Others were flashing different signs they had made. I knew then that this was the real deal. I had seen it on TV but there was nothing like being a part of the atmosphere in person. We finally made it to the line and there were literally thousands of people out there. Some had lawn chairs with them and others had sleeping bags because they had camped out the night before. The media was out in full force and cameras from various stations where all over the place. I had never seen anything like it. As I looked and listened to some of the singers, I could tell that they had real talent. Once we made it inside, everyone took a seat. It was amazing to me to see the amount of people who came out. I also had never been in the Georgia Dome so it was a doubly fun experience. I didn't even know what song I was going to sing. I knew I would try my best.

At the Georgia Dome, I simply let loose and had a good time. They played music and everyone was enjoying the atmosphere. It was like the registration was a huge event in itself. After a little while, they announced that it would be time to start the auditions. I came to find out that this was only the first round of auditions and you would actually be auditioning in front of talent scouts and producers for the show. We were lined up on the field in groups of four and there were about fifteen tables where producers and scouts were sitting to judge us. Everyone would step up to the table one at a time and sing a song. If they liked you, they gave you a yellow ticket to come back for the next round of auditions. When it was my turn, I had decided I would sing one of my favorite songs, A Thousand Miles by Vanessa Carlton. It was symbolic to me. I felt like I had walked a thousand miles to get to this point in my life. I stepped up, spinned around and started singing for them. I had a big radiant smile. I wanted to make them laugh and I thought they loved it. I was the last one from my group to sing and I went back to the line. The producers started talking amongst each other and in a few minutes they called three people up to the table from our group. I was left back at the line. I figured they didn't choose me. In spite of this, I felt good. The next thing I knew, one of the producers told them they didn't make it. She called me up to the table and told me I had made it to the next round of auditions. I was shocked and beside myself. They handed me a yellow ticket that confirmed it. They took me back to a room to take a picture and fill out a bit of paperwork. It stated I would come back to the audition next month. I couldn't believe it. This was exactly the boost I needed to start feeling better.

That month passed by rather quickly and before I knew it, it was time for the next round of auditions. I got a chance to see everyone who had made it to the next round of the selection process. I took the same approach that I had for the last round, just to be myself and have fun. A lot of people there were very serious and acted as if their lives depended on making it on the show. There were definitely a number of good singers there so I knew I would have to entertain the judges in order to get consideration. They said this would be the last round before you could see Randy, Paula, and Simon. There had to be more than two hundred people in attendance for this round. I waited for a few hours this time before I was finally able to go in front of the producers. I did the exact same thing I did the first time. I really wanted to make it so I gave it my best effort. When I was done, they conferred with themselves. A few minutes later, one of the producers came to talk to me. "We think that you have a lot of energy and that you are very entertaining." "Congratulations!" He said that I made it to the judges. I would get my chance to go in front of Randy, Paula, and Simon. I jumped up and down and was so happy. That was really a good day for me and I felt better from that day forth. I was no longer feeling down and out. Just this little event was enough of a spark to make me feel better. That audition would be the next day. I told SirTavion about it and he couldn't believe it. He was so happy for me and proud of me for doing something I wanted to do. He knew about me pursuing Top Model and he was glad to see me able to bounce back and do something else. That night, I went to sleep with my mind full of anxiety and excitement.

The next day had a much smaller crowd than before. There were maybe seventy people this time. Out of the original fifteen thousand that had tried out for their audition, there was only a remnant remaining. At this point, I anticipated seeing the judges, especially my favorite one Simon Cowell. I was ready to get it done. My nerves were very jittery and the only way to end it was to go in front of them. I had to wait a few hours before it was my turn. Finally, my moment had arrived. I walked into the audition room and saw the three judges sitting there waiting for me to sing. I came in and I still couldn't believe it. Being there in person was entirely different than seeing them on TV. I really wanted to do well and impress them. I wanted to go to Hollywood and have shot. Why not? I had made it this far. "What's your name honey?" Paula asked me. "My name's Eva." I replied. It was so funny that I was talking to her. *"Oh my goodness. I need to calm down."* I thought internally. "What makes you think you're the next American idol?" Simon asked me. I replied with confidence that I felt I had the look, the voice, the presence, everything. "Good girl" he said. "What are you going to sing Eva?" he asked. "I'm going to sing Vanessa Carlton's A Thousand Miles" I said. "Off you go then!" he replied. From there, I gave my performance. I belted out the lyrics and tried to entertain the judges at the same time when the impossible happened. My sticker had fallen off my dress and landed on the floor. Before I knew it, I had stepped on the sticker and slipped on the ground. I couldn't believe this was actually happening. Internally I was a mess however I didn't show it. I was so embarrassed. *"I can not believe I just slipped in front of the judges."* I kept telling myself. I wanted to get up and run out of the room and cry yet I resolved to regain my composure. I wanted to show everyone that might see this, if you fall down you can get back up and try again. I also wanted to express to everyone that I didn't mean to fall and that was not part of my audition. I got back up and finished singing. Simon didn't believe me. He truly thought it was an act. I tried to tell all the judges that I didn't mean to fall and that it wasn't staged. I didn't fall in any of the previous auditions. Everything happens for a reason though. I had an awesome time and had a chance to enjoy the whole experience from the very beginning. At least I had made it that far.

Four months later, the show aired. I didn't know if they would show me on TV or not. I told everyone I knew that I had been in front of the judges and that there was a chance I could be on. They all said they would look out for me. It felt good to have support from everyone. Even my family in California said that they would be watching.

During that time I talked to the family in California a few more times and I discovered that I had family in Columbus, Georgia. That was the city my family was from and Jeannie originally lived in before moving to out west. I went and met some of them and we hit it off immediately. They also said they would be watching. I got a chance to talk to my other aunt as well. Her presence was very inviting and she gave me further insight into who Jeannie was. She told me a lot of good things about her, including the fact that she used to do hair. I now know from whom I received that talent from. It felt so good to have a support system from my real family. It was an indescribable feeling and it shows me how important having family really can be. It just so happened that *American Idol* decided to give me my own segment in the show. I couldn't believe that over thirty million viewers across the nation saw me fall flat on my behind. Other than that, I enjoyed being on television. It was something I had wanted to do for a very long time and I finally got a chance to fulfill that dream also. My life was headed in an upward direction again and I already felt as if I had progressed greatly from where I had been. I enjoyed this feeling. I was sober as well and had not backslid at all. I knew I was blessed.

CHAPTER 23
Peace of Mind

After *American Idol*, I got very busy for a little while. I even made couple of appearances here and there and had a couple of radio interviews. I enjoyed it and handled it well. I wasn't a star, just a girl who got an opportunity to be on television and I wanted to turn it into a positive situation. Even to this day, people ask me if I was that girl on *American Idol* who sang Vanessa Carlton. They say they have seen my video on YouTube. I just tell them I was thankful for the experience. I really enjoyed everything.

I was feeling a lot better and lot a more fulfilled. Things in my life were stable although I missed both of my mothers tremendously. During this time, I really started connect with the family that was here in Columbus. I had some cousins who lived there. They were my Uncle Sidney's daughters and they all made me feel so warm and welcome. They immediately accepted me and I love them for that. Getting to know my family history was invaluable. There was so much I wanted to know.

One day I received a letter in the mail from someone in my family announcing that we were having a family get together. It would be the first time in our family history that we would be having some sort of a reunion. I found this to be very interesting because that meant many people in our family would be meeting for the first time. We would be meeting in Senoia, Georgia. I was so happy because I had not met many others yet beyond those in Columbus and it would be the perfect opportunity to do so. I thanked the Most High. He had brought me back to them at just the right time. It was a point in time in my life is which I was happy. I would have a chance to finally meet my entire family. I couldn't have even imagined a year ago that this would be happening. I found out that the family in California was going to attend. I would finally see my big sister and younger brother face to face for the very first time. I cannot explain how excited I was about this. When SirTavion got home, I told him about the reunion and he was very happy for me. He said that he would definitely go and support. I had so much running through my mind. I was really apprehensive about meeting them all. I just wanted them to accept me for who I was.

Speaking of families, little did I know that I was actually about to be starting one of my own. A few weeks after receiving the letter about the family gathering, I started to feel sick every day. Before I knew it, I was taking a pregnancy test. The results came back positive. I was going to be a mother. SirTavion and I were going to have a child together. I told him the news and I don't know if I've ever seen him smile as much I did when I told him I was pregnant. He was very happy and I knew he was going to be a terrific father. He told me that he was happy that I was carrying his child and that he had confidence that I would be a good mother. I was glad to hear that from him. That was very important to me. Here I was, about to start a family of my own. I told all of my family and friends.

A couple of months passed by and before I knew it, the day of the reunion had arrived. I woke up that morning full of emotions. It would be an unforgettable day. We got dressed and left home. It would be about a two-hour trip. On the way, my heart started beating faster and faster the closer we got. My mind raced with so many thoughts of the past and the present. I was glad I had SirTavion there with me. We found the neighborhood where the house was and coasted down the street. We saw a large house over the horizon that had decorations and balloons on the mailbox. We knew then that we were there. We pulled up to the house and parked. I sat there in the car and took a deep breath. SirTavion grabbed my hand and asked "Baby are you ready for this?" I looked him in the eye and said "I've been waiting for this moment my entire life."

Finally, after long years of turmoil and adversity I stood on the cusp of a new life, a life no longer filled with secrets, deception, and manipulation. No longer was my life a secret to even myself. The mysteries of my life had finally begun to unravel while being replaced with truth and peace. I had attained an entirely different level of peace in my life. I had a good man in my life and we were starting our own family. Here I was, two years completely removed from the club and drugs and my life was in a much better place. A place it had never been before at any point in my life. I was thankful that God had allowed me a chance to live happily and peacefully. I could now use my story as an inspiration. I was living proof that you can persevere and make it. Your dreams can come true too. Never give up on yourself. I am living proof that you can fall down and get back up. Don't ever lie down.

As we sat in the car, it was time to go inside and SirTavion came over to my door and let me out. We got out of the car and walked toward the house. I knew that once I opened that door, everything would change forever. With so many doors being closed in my life, it was a phenomenal feeling to finally open one.

Acknowledgments

God I would like to thank you for being in my life and saving me. I would like to acknowledge my fiancé SirTavion McGhee for supporting my dreams and helping me with this book. I also want to let all of the people out there in the world who are adopted or have never met your parents that you are not alone. I understand how you feel. No matter how bad times might be right now, it will get better. I want to thank all of my fans, and friends and family. My friends mean so much to me and I would like to thanks them. Dontee Hubbard, Wynnette Santos, Kristal Lightning-Dyson, George Byrd, Malinda Williams, Eric Miller, Chassidy Thomason, Paula Jones, Barbara McGhee, Patricia Tarver, Joe Patterson, Mandisa Williams, Kristina Mcguire, and I also want to thank American Idol for giving me my time to shine. Everyone who went out and bought this book, I'd like to thank you too. Thanks to all my friends in Hamilton, Ohio and Blountstown, Florida that helped create these memories. I can't forget Myspace.com. I found my sister on your networking site. Thanks Tom! I want to also thank FAMU for giving me a chance. Thanks also to Vision Photography. I have to thank the City of Atlanta for showing me so much love.

Manufactured By: RR Donnelley
                     Breinigsville, PA USA
                     September, 2010